Natural Rest for Addiction

A Revolutionary Way to Recover Through Presence

Scott Kiloby

Cover Design by Benjamin Cziller, www.imagedriven.com

Back Cover Photo by Emily Goodman

ISBN: **1-4818-3908-X**
ISBN 13: **9781481839082**

FOREWORD

What is spiritual awakening? And how is it relevant to recovery from addiction?

There are so many books on the subjects of self-improvement, self-help, spiritual awakening, and addiction recovery available these days. So many methods, practices, programs, teachers and teachings that often seem so very different, even contradictory. So many people promising us so much, and it can all be so confusing for someone who is genuinely open to discovering true peace and rest in their lives.

There are so many questions...

Which method works best?

Can I just stop using my drug of choice without support from others or the help of a method?

How do I know when I'm recovering from addiction?

Is recovery just about being abstinent? Or is it something more than that?

Is spiritual awakening what I need to overcome addiction?

Is spiritual awakening an 'event' that happens to some people and not to others?

Is awakening something that can be reached through methods at all?

It can get so exhausting, trying to figure all of this out with the poor little mind! But *Natural Rest for Addiction* clears away our confusion. If you are looking for a way to overcome addiction that is simple, accessible and practical yet deeply penetrating, then this book stands out from the crowd.

I have known Scott for many years now. He is a teacher who does not simply regurgitate concepts that he has learned from others. His words have been uniquely forged in the fire of his own pain. He speaks with authenticity and integrity from his own deepest experience, and teaches not by trying to be a teacher, but by being a living example of what he teaches. He is a rare breed—a teacher who actually lives and breathes his own message.

Scott speaks of recovery from addiction through spiritual awakening. But he expresses his message in such a practical, down-to-earth way that at first you may not even realize you're reading a book about spiritual awakening! His words carry deep wisdom, but he avoids all those heavy, esoteric concepts found in the ancient scriptures and traditions. He also doesn't overload you with mountains of intellectual knowledge about the science of addiction, but gently takes you by the proverbial hand and shows you a way out of the insanity of the mind, and its endless seeking for something more in the future. Through clear explanations and piercing inquiries, he shows you that the present moment is always, always the key to recovery. And he shows you how safe it is to dive headfirst into the moment, and to stay there. His method is a truly living meditation that you can take with you into every moment of your life.

Scott points you to the discovery of who you really are, beyond who you think you are—a vast, quiet, non-dual ocean of present-moment awareness that deeply and unconditionally welcomes all thoughts, sensations and emotions, all energies of life, as they arise and dissolve in you. When you cease identifying as a limited, deficient and separate 'self' looking for freedom and peace in a future moment, you recognize the freedom that exists here and now, the very last place you'd ever think to look! Make no mistake, this book will challenge your assumptions about addiction and recovery. And it will also challenge many of your deeply-held beliefs about yourself and the world around you. Be prepared to let go of some of your cherished concepts about life!

Despite what common sense and conventional wisdom tell us, it is actually incredibly healing to stop running away from present-moment pain and discomfort, and to just sit with those energies as they come up in you, to welcome them as friends that are trying to help you or even awaken you, rather than enemies that are trying to destroy you. However strange it may sound, much of our suffering comes not directly from our pain and discomfort, but from our attempts to escape that pain and discomfort in the moment.

Most of us attempt to distract ourselves from pain, or numb ourselves to it, or avoid, transcend or even destroy it. We do this through thinking, through ingesting drugs, alcohol, or other chemicals, through shopping, working, gambling, or sex, through seeking external validation or love, through seeking money, success, self-improvement, enlightenment, or even through seeking future recovery. As this cycle of seeking pleasure and avoiding pain takes over, it begins to run our lives. We end up swinging wildly between these polarities, caught in a continuous search for something more, never finding an end to this cycle, often feeling far away from true peace and contentment and love.

Scott painstakingly points out the futility of always seeking to escape what is. Drawing from his own experience with addiction and years of working with others, he points to resting in presence, allowing ourselves to feel whatever we feel, even if what we feel is deeply uncomfortable, intense or even painful. He shows us how to allow all thoughts, all feelings, all bodily energies, positive and negative, light and dark, to just be there, as they are, and to relax into the wide open space that holds them. He points repetitively to this 'resting' throughout the book, with good reason. We don't always hear or understand this approach the first time round, or even the second or third time. It sometimes takes a degree of repetition for us to see in our own experience the sheer futility of escaping, and how the escaping is the problem, not the solution. To the mind, Scott's approach may seem upside-down or backwards, even a little bit crazy. But then, as Scott reminds us, you are not the mind at all.

Some religions and spiritual ideologies promise a future time, perhaps after death, where all discomfort will be swept away. Our parents, out of love, tried to protect us from feeling discomfort in the first place. The entertainment industry turns our attention away from discomfort every day. The advertising industry feeds on our discomfort and dissatisfaction with the way things are. Some self-improvement methods just give us new ways to escape dissatisfaction, thereby making an enemy out of it. Some teachings or methods even tell us that there is something wrong with us if we experience 'negative' energies at all!

From all sides we receive the basic message that there is something wrong with us, that we are not okay as we are unless we are feeling 100% perfect and comfortable and secure and happy all the time. We are led to believe that we are deficient or broken in some basic way, that we are fallen sinners, that we are psychologically unsound, that we are even beyond repair. We are conditioned to believe we are addicts and always will be. From all sides we get the same message: YOU ARE NOT GOOD ENOUGH. And so addictive seeking becomes the constant companion of our lives.

Nobody has ever shown us how to be with discomfort, how to welcome it in, how to say 'yes' to the uncomfortable energies of life, how to stop identifying with them, so they release naturally and effortlessly. But Scott shows us how. He constantly reminds us that there is nothing wrong with us, and never was. He shows us that, at the most fundamental level, we are deeply okay as we are. At the very core of our being, there is a wholeness that cannot be put into words, an inner silence, a deep stillness that just got a little bit neglected over the years and needs some new friendship. Through his teachings, we come to recognize ourselves as the perfect calm in the midst of the storm of life, the natural rest that never, ever leaves, even when things on the surface do not seem so restful.

I am amazed at Scott's ability to bring the ancient teachings of spiritual awakening down from the mountaintops, onto the streets, into the room that you are in, into your heart and into the deepest, darkest recesses of your intimate personal experience. He fearlessly shines light into addiction's darkest hiding places, and guides you towards an ever-present freedom the likes of which you never imagined possible.

Above all else, this teaching frees you from something that is at the core of all addictions—your addiction to self.

This is a truly wonderful book, and it's likely to reach people who have never before been reached by this kind of work. May you discover the rest that you have always longed for—the rest that you already are. I leave you in Scott's capable, trustworthy, and experienced hands.

Jeff Foster
Author of The Deepest Acceptance
www.lifewithoutacentre.com

Table of Contents

My Story

For twenty years, I lived in addiction.

My addiction progressed from smoking marijuana as a teenager to drinking lots of alcohol and using many drugs including methamphetamine, cocaine, and LSD later in life.

Near the end of this dark cycle of using, I was swallowing handfuls of prescription painkillers, several times a day. Addiction crawled into every area of my life. I found myself caught in addictive patterns related to money, food, relationships, sex, success, attention, and acknowledgment. (And that's just the short list.) I hid my addiction from everyone, ashamed of what my life had become.

Through the help of wonderfully supportive family members and a recovery program, I was able to quit using drugs and alcohol. Yet, the addictive cycle continued in more "socially acceptable" ways, such as trying to control and change others, embarking on a constant desire for self-improvement, and finally, the quest for spiritual enlightenment.

I searched through many self-help, positive thinking, religious, and spiritual programs. I read tons of books, watched many videos, and followed the works of a long list of teachers. I was hunting for healing but nothing seemed to provide permanent release. I'd make a little progress here and there, in terms of reducing the addictive seeking, but even my desire to end my addiction became an addiction.

Through the help of some wise teachers and an intention to look more deeply into my experience of presence, I finally found the key . . .

Freedom from addiction is already contained in the one place an addict refuses to look—the present moment.

This changed everything! I discovered that by simply resting in presence repeatedly throughout the day and allowing all thoughts, emotions, cravings, and other energies to be just as they are, the addictive cycle eventually releases itself and falls away. The freedom I'd ached for couldn't be found in my own life story (the past) or any future event that I had to someday reach.

I saw that freedom from addiction was already here, contained perfectly within presence itself.

For three years, I kept quiet about this treasure. Because "natural rest" has to be *experienced* rather than only understood by the mind, it took me awhile to find the right words to share it with others. Finally, one day in early 2010, these words came. Actually, they gushed out of me like a heavy downpour of rain in early spring. The result is here in this book. It's my gift to you—whoever you are, wherever you are.

If you're suffering now or have ever suffered with addiction, please take this gift and experience the natural release of addiction in the one place you likely haven't looked—the here and now!

Find the healing that's already inside us all,

–Scott Kiloby

Introduction

Have you been chasing the future?

Are you constantly looking for the next fix, the next high? Are you always looking for something else, something more?

Does the *present moment* feel as though it's missing something?

Does it feel like you can't find the complete satisfaction you're seeking, no matter how much you look for it in the future?

. . . No matter how many drugs you take or drinks you drink?
. . . No matter how much "stuff" you buy?
. . . No matter how much you work?
. . . No matter how many experiences you have?
. . . No matter how much love or sex you get?
. . . No matter how much you gamble or eat?

If you answered "yes" to any of these, you may be suffering from addiction.

Whether it's a full-blown heroin fix or an inability to stop scarfing down cookies, addiction has a way of controlling our lives. It sets us on a course of constant, uncontrollable seeking toward the *next* moment.

As addicts we seek to avoid any unpleasant, painful feelings and thoughts appearing *now*. These are remnants of the past. We unconsciously carry them with us and erroneously believe that the future will somehow set us free. We keep searching for a release from our past emotional and psychological pain as well as any feelings of lack, restlessness, or boredom. In our addiction, there's no such thing as "enough." We just keep seeking, and seeking, and seeking. Yet, *never* finding . . .

Addiction is the gaping hole in our lives that can never be filled.

No matter how much we keep seeking the future, we never find the end of the seeking thread. In our addiction, we may find moments of release or brief periods of satisfaction because we've temporarily quenched our urges, but we never find that ongoing, permanent release from the seeking cycle.

These brief moments inevitably fade because *all* experiences are temporary.

In not finding the lasting freedom we crave, we suffer further, which only causes us to seek into the future more and more. It's a never-ending cycle.

So . . . what's the key to freedom from addiction?

Natural Rest.

Natural Rest cannot be understood by the mind; it can only be experienced.

As addicts, we're addicted to *thinking* that the future will give us satisfaction. But the problem is, addiction to thinking can never be released through more thinking. Addicts often overlook the natural rest of the present moment, which only perpetuates the cycle of addiction.

You won't be able to rely on thinking to find your way into natural rest. Instead, this book will take you on a journey where you can actually *experience* natural rest for yourself.

Natural rest is found in the present moment—a place where we're not emphasizing or obsessing on our thoughts. This rest is "natural" because it's already here for us. It's the felt sense of *presence.* All we have to do is relax into it on a repeated basis.

This book invites you to begin one simple practice: *the practice of repeatedly relaxing into a state of thought-free rest in the present moment.*

Relaxing into the natural rest of the present moment is an incredible opportunity for healing any addiction. At first, the practice may seem difficult. We may experience a mind that's frantically busy, a chattering mind that just wants to continuously think about the past or the future.

In the beginning, we may experience only short glimpses of restful, thought-free presence. But over time, the practice of continuously resting will become automatic and natural.

Presence is right here, right now.

Presence is not a contrived belief system.

It's not a program in which you have to convince yourself of certain mental viewpoints. It's not a complicated manual about how to live your life. It's not a code of conduct that you memorize and take with you everywhere you go. It's not a set of affirmations that you have to frequently repeat. It's not dependent on positive thinking strategies.

Presence is much simpler and more immediate than any of this.

Presence is our natural way of being in the here and now without emphasizing our stories as completely true and real. Stories may still arise, but they begin to feel lighter and more transparent. This way of being is always and already available in each moment. Once we recognize this, the cycle of addiction can finally begin to relax!

Other recovery programs provide only temporary thinking strategies to keep addicts from relapse. Some programs involve taking medications or use other methods and technologies that deal mainly with the *symptoms* of addiction (i.e., cravings) or focus only on certain areas in an addict's life where seeking is present.

Some programs speak of spiritual awakening, but then tend to keep us addictively seeking the future for our awakening, constantly focused on ourselves in a self-centered way. Other programs are based solely on belief systems. This is fine. But if an addict doesn't believe in the tenets of that system, he or she cannot find lasting help.

These programs are important contributions to recovery from addiction. They've helped many people. But they don't address the root cause of the addiction cycle—the addict herself. The addict is an insatiable seeker, and the seeker is the story of self—one that addictively looks for satisfaction in the future—but never truly finds it.

In natural rest, we see through the seeker identity itself. This thoroughly releases the mental and emotional seeking energy within us.

By resting in presence on a repeated basis, we naturally stop seeking the future. In no longer looking to the future, this natural, restful presence begins to permeate every part of our lives, providing rest, freedom, and well-being in all the areas where we've been trapped by the cycle of addictive seeking.

Natural rest is authentic spiritual awakening, which is the only thing that can truly uproot addiction. Addiction is the fundamental seeking energy that has been our constant companion in life, leading us to feel an ongoing sense of incompleteness that propels us constantly toward the future.

Restful, natural presence holds incredible transformative power for us. It eases cravings, anxiety, obsession, seeking energy, and clinging to self-centered thoughts and emotions.

Aren't we seeking peace of mind?

Most of the time, we don't even know *what* we're seeking or *why*. We just know that an uncontrollable urge arises within to look for something else, something more, in the very next moment. The restless mind is our constant companion.

But by resting repeatedly into the present moment, we can begin to find *what* we're seeking. In a flash, it becomes clear.

As addicts, what we're seeking more than anything else is the end of the seeking itself. We're looking for our minds to rest, so we can enjoy life in the present moment.

By repeatedly relaxing into the present moment, we can find the end of seeking. It's right here, right now, in the one place we've been overlooking: *this moment!*

Once the seeking falls away, the positive attributes of peace, compassion, love, ease, freedom, and well-being arise naturally. By relaxing repeatedly into the natural rest of the present moment, we come to see that these attributes are not things we acquire in time, but inherent attributes of our own restful nature.

Rest is everyone's untapped resource.

Rest exists within each and every person who has ever suffered from addiction. Rest is the natural, relaxed, thought-free space of the present moment.

This thought-free space isn't a space in which we're suddenly unable to function nor is it ever a space where we lose the ability to use our thoughts for practical purposes, such as learning how to use new computer software, performing a task at work, teaching your child how to read, making a grocery list, remembering to take out the trash, paying your bills, taking the steps to save money for retirement, communicating better with your spouse, joining a cause to help others, and on and on and on.

Through resting in presence, incredible wisdom arises, and within this natural wisdom, the self-seeking aspect of thought simply quiets and falls to the side. The self-seeking aspect of thought has little practical value. It's based on a constant sense of personal lack that we carry with us. In presence, we find a sense of completion that dissolves this self-seeking.

Presence is like a buried treasure waiting to be discovered right in your own backyard. In fact, it's even closer than that. It's already within you. And, this book holds the key to uncovering that treasure.

An addict can spend an entire lifetime looking for such a treasure in drugs, alcohol, shopping, gambling, relationships, material goods, sex, thinking, spiritual experiences, or any number of other substances or activities.

But the movement to seek this treasure in things and future events is actually a movement to escape the treasure that's already *here*.

By now, you may have some obvious, skeptical questions, such as . . .

. . . Can it be this easy?
. . . Can the answer to addiction be within me already?
. . . Can it really be in the here and now?

Yes! This is the great news. On the other hand, we're not saying, "You're already free." Such an assertion would be detrimental to anyone already caught up in the energy of seeking because it would give that person a false sense of mental certainty.

Mental certainty about *anything* will never deliver stable, ongoing rest. The certainty of natural rest is *experiential,* so to know directly its transformative power, you must come to experience this rest for yourself.

Although this treasure lies in the natural rest of the present moment, remember: addiction is the constant movement to escape from the present moment and the uncomfortable thoughts and feelings of the past.

You want to deal directly with this movement of escaping so you can shine a light on it and investigate it.

By noticing the thoughts and feelings that make you want to escape into the future, you will gain tremendous insight. Through this insight, it will become easier to relax into natural and effortless presence.

Natural Rest: A Few Introductory Points

The following section is a summary of the content of this book. We invite you to just take a look through these points to get a better sense of natural rest. Each chapter that follows goes into greater detail.

Defining Addiction and Recovery

The term addiction is used in this book in the broadest sense. We define addiction as the repetitive, compulsive need for and use of anything including any substance or activity.

Substances include alcohol, drugs, food, or any other substance that alters one's mood once it enters the body, creating a desire to use the substance repeatedly. This includes binging.

Activities include gambling, work, sex, the Internet, pornography, seeking self-improvement or spiritual awakening, or any other activity that results in a compulsion to engage in the activity repeatedly.

Addiction includes compulsively emphasizing thought for a sense of self. For this reason, virtually all humans are addicts, regardless of whether they've experienced the habitual tendency to use addictive substances.

Addiction is often accompanied by the sense of having little to no control over the desire to use the substance or engage in the activity. Addiction often negatively affects many areas of our lives including our mental, emotional and physical health, relationships, families, and work, as well as larger aspects of society including our health care and legal systems.

In natural rest, recovery is found through present moment awareness.

Natural rest is not a method based on self-improvement. It's not aimed at improving the sense of self through striving toward the future. Instead, recovery is based on seeing through the ego or sense of self that lives in our thoughts of past and future. In this way of recovery, seeking a more improved sense of self over time is considered just *another* form of addictive seeking.

The Central Practice

This book is an ongoing invitation for us to relax repeatedly, throughout the day, in the spacious rest of the present moment. This restful presence is available to us in every situation of life—not only when we're sitting or physically still. We can access this rest even when we're physically active.

Natural rest is never dependent on any particular condition or situation. It's available in every moment of our lives. All we have to do is *choose* to rest in presence as often as possible.

In addiction, we have spent so much time and energy trying to escape the present moment. The choice to rest in presence repeatedly throughout the day is the most important choice we can make. It's the key to our freedom from the cycle of addiction.

Although resting in presence is the central practice of this book, the Living Inquiries are indispensable tools in the Natural Rest way of recovery. They uproot long-held stories that keep us reaching for substances and activities for relief. The Compulsion Inquiry, by itself, is a powerful way to dissolve compulsive thoughts and feelings as soon as they arise. You will find the Living Inquiries in Chapter Seven.

All Energies Are Equal

We come to see all energies as equal movements within our awareness. You will see the term "energies" defined differently in various places in this book. In the broadest sense, the term includes anything that comes and goes temporarily within our awareness (e.g., thoughts, emotions, sensations, sights, sounds, smells, tastes, states, experiences, cravings, and behaviors). But to keep it simple, consider energies to be basically three things: words, pictures and bodily energy.

Whenever you see the term "thoughts" in the book, know that it is referring to the words and mental pictures that arise and fall in your mind. And, although the terms "emotions" and "sensations" are used throughout the book to describe what we feel in the body, notice that emotions and sensations are just bodily energy when they aren't being labeled. Breaking our experience down to these simple components (words, pictures and bodily energy) makes this book easier to read and makes the Living Inquiries in Chapter Seven easier to do.

Seeing all energies as equal allows addictive thoughts and behaviors to come to rest as we stop emphasizing energies that make us feel good while simultaneously avoiding or trying to escape energies that make us feel bad.

Before we are introduced to this way of rest, stories and traumas from the past, fearful thoughts and emotions about the future, and other ongoing mental and emotional disturbances seem to remain with us. They lie dormant, but are regularly triggered in a way that leads us to reach outside ourselves for relief through substances and activities.

Through resting in presence, we rely less and less on our story for a sense of self. We're finally able to see and face the energies that we've been trying to escape. In this restful seeing, we realize that all energies are equal. To say "all energies are equal" doesn't mean that we stop feeling emotions and thinking thoughts. And, it doesn't mean that all thoughts and emotions are experienced as the same.

To say "all energies are equal" is to say that they're seen to be equally temporary. Each energy movement does the same thing: it appears, hangs around awhile, and then disappears, leaving no trace. Energies begin leaving no trace as we experience them arising and falling within an impersonal, indestructible presence—rather than within a personal story. As we see for ourselves that all thoughts and emotions are equal energies, coming and going within a perfectly stable presence, we begin to experience mental and emotional balance in our lives.

In relaxing repeatedly into the present moment, we come to see that each energy movement appears and disappears *equally* within restful presence. The constant emphasis on these energies naturally comes to rest. Seeking actually ends!

No Energy Movement Is Emphasized

In this way of natural rest, we don't emphasize any movement of energy. To emphasize any movement of energy would make it more important than simply resting in presence.

Examples of emphasizing energies include trying to add to, change, analyze, overcome, suppress, or get rid of thoughts, emotions, cravings, sensations, states, experiences, or any other movement. The invitation is to see that *all* energy movements are equal and, as each energy rises and falls, to not emphasize any of it.

By simply choosing to relax repeatedly into the present moment and allowing all energies to simply come and go without emphasizing them, we can discover an equanimity, peace, and freedom that permeate every moment.

Whenever we emphasize energy movements versus relaxing into the natural rest of presence—the self-centered personal will is acting. This self-centeredness and its need to control and manipulate life only keeps us trapped in addictive tendencies and seeking the future.

In natural rest, when any movement of energy arises, we don't try to change it or push it away. We allow it to be exactly as it is. Then we relax into the still, quiet presence that reveals itself naturally whenever the movement comes to rest.

This presence contains all the transformative power we're seeking.

There's no need to apply any effort. At the end of each movement of effort, we will notice the space as it reveals itself. Then we will take a moment and rest *as that space.* We will do this repeatedly throughout the day, whenever we can.

In resting there, we will see that all movements of energy are temporary. Each movement comes to rest on its own, back into the natural rest of the present moment. Addiction has controlled our lives precisely because we've been emphasizing certain movements (e.g., seeking energy) rather than relaxing into the present moment.

When we stop adding any energy to a movement, it naturally loses its fuel, and our self-centeredness, addictive cravings, and obsessions lose their fuel as well. They simply no longer haunt us or control our lives.

As energies arise and fall seamlessly within the natural rest of presence, we come to see that all movements of energy are infused with rest. In this realization, a new kind of potential will arise—a selfless, restful, creative one.

This is where our true power lies!

Rest Naturally Releases Self-Centeredness

We have suffered as addicts because of our self-centeredness. Natural rest is not a method by which we assert our personal will in order to overcome self-centeredness. That circular type of reasoning doesn't work. The personal will can never get rid of itself. We can never make rest a future goal because that would only be another act of our personal will—and recovery would become the new drug to chase. It would only engage the self-centered seeking energy that lies at the core of our addiction in the first place.

Instead, we will notice that, when we simply relax into the natural rest of the present moment, self-centered viewpoints come to rest naturally, effortlessly.

Our lives no longer feel contrived, conditioned, or divided. They no longer feel dominated by a sense of self that's based in lack. As a result, seeking toward future finally comes to rest.

Natural rest has a profound impact on our self-centeredness. We discover that presence is the hidden treasure within us. Whenever we see a self-centered movement, we simply rest in presence. It's truly that simple!

Presence effortlessly transforms self-centered energy into restful, selfless energy. And, as this rest naturally releases our self-centeredness, we experience a natural desire to be of service to others.

We discover our newfound creativity, wisdom, and compassion.

Experiential Certainty

We come to realize that no words can ever convince us that resting in the present moment is the key to recovery.

We must experience this rest for ourselves.

Through repeated personal experience, we will become certain of this rest and that it's the key to our recovery. An unshakable knowing occurs versus a belief or thought.

We don't *believe in* rest. We don't emphasize mental viewpoints about rest. We simply notice that rest *is* already here . . . and that it's the treasure we've been seeking all along. It's ours to discover. No one can talk us into it. Yet, once it's discovered, no one can talk us out of it. It's that stable and certain.

A Participatory Way of Recovery

Natural rest is a participatory way of recovery that values involvement at a group level, including the importance of relationship, mutual support, equality, diversity, dialogue, and inclusiveness. All voices are welcome in Natural Rest meetings. In this book, the "we" pronoun is used to designate the importance of relationships and mutual support in recovery.

Mutual support and participation at the group level is beneficial for addicts. Simply being around others who are discovering the benefit of presence is contagious. Mutual support and participation also help us avoid isolation. Isolation can lead to loneliness, depression, and even relapse.

We are encouraged to remain in contact with each other. We do this through Natural Rest group meetings and/or one-on-one contact between participants.

With Natural Rest group meetings, our intent is to form safe places, both online and in our local communities, for those who are ready to find recovery through presence.

These meetings are places where people can share their experiences and ask for the guidance of those who have a more direct experience of relaxing into the natural rest of the present moment.

This book uses simple language in order to reach as many people as possible. The language is also designed to avoid conflict between varying belief systems, religions, philosophies, and worldviews.

All belief systems, religions, philosophies, and worldviews are absolutely welcome here. But we also ask that no one impose his or her viewpoint on another. No mental viewpoint is absolutized here.

To absolutize (dictate) a viewpoint is to make it into absolute truth and mentally emphasize it above all others. This can only lead to a rigid sense of separation between us. When we separate ourselves from one another by absolutizing or dictating a viewpoint, we lose sight of what this way of recovery is really about—finding recovery through presence. Mutual support works best when we release the idea of being right and focus instead on being of service to each other.

Any insights gained through resting are valuable. Insights open us up to resting more fully. We share our insights as a service to others, whenever such service is requested. We *don't* impose our viewpoints on others. We see that insights and viewpoints can be helpful, but they're poor substitutes for experientially resting in presence.

Our only interest is mutually supporting each other to realize the natural benefits of resting in presence.

Attachment to Recovery Programs and the Addict Identity

Natural rest reveals a release from self-centered attachments, including any attachment to any recovery program. We don't come to this way of recovery to find an identity on the individual level. We don't come here to become dependent on this method for life. In the natural rest of presence, dependency—in *all* its forms—releases itself.

We may use the term "addict" or "recovering addict" as a conventional label to refer to someone who is or has been suffering from addiction or is finding recovery. Yet we don't emphasize any label to define a sense of self. All mental labels are considered to be equal movements of energy here.

Presence releases the need to identify with thought.

Identifying heavily with mental labels can create the "mentality of sickness" where we feel trapped in a conceptual box as a "sick person." These labels set us apart from society. When we insist on these labels, we're asking society to treat us as damaged goods or second-class citizens.

Identifying with these labels can close the mind and leave us unable to think freshly and creatively about addiction and recovery. It may also cut us off from interacting with others in society who don't share that label.

Identifying with labels such as "addict" and "recovering addict" can set us apart from our families and friends, making us feel special and different. This only strengthens self-centered thinking. Then we become more interested in strengthening and maintaining this identity instead of finding true spiritual awakening that can free us from identifying with all limiting conceptual labels.

Such identification can lead to ethno-centric thinking where addicts or recovering addicts, as a group, set themselves apart from other groups and from society in general. This can lead to conflict and division. We can become more interested in strengthening the group identity than in realizing the limitation of all conceptual identities.

Group identities can limit the freedom of a group to be open to change as well as to all kinds of people. The moment a group takes on a conceptual identity, it closes its doors to thousands of others who might benefit from being involved in that group, but who cannot—for whatever reason—fit themselves within that restrictive label.

This way of recovery is about experientially resting in the present moment as often as possible. That's all. It's not a cult. We're *not* seeking identity on a collective level here.

This is a support system based on a simple invitation to rest in presence. Identifying oneself with a conceptual label isn't necessary nor is it desired. Anyone wanting freedom from the cycle of addiction is welcome here.

In this way of rest, we're interested in complete liberation, including freedom from any thought patterns that create and maintain division and separation in our lives, on *any* level.

Natural Rest Groups and Servants

You may find an already-established group of people in your area that have joined together to help each other with this way of recovery from addiction. This is called a "Natural Rest Group." You may form a group in your area if one is not established already.

If Natural Rest groups are formed, they should contain elected "servants" who help to conduct the meetings and take care of the administrative needs of the group. Servants should be people who have direct experience with the benefit of presence as it pertains to recovery. They should be available in meetings and one-on-one settings and act as mentors for those who are new to this way of dealing with addiction.

Visit www.naturalrestforaddiction.com to find or establish a Natural Rest Group in your area.

Anonymity and Confidentiality

We never share names of those participating in meetings with anyone outside the group. Whatever's shared within a meeting by anyone is considered confidential.

This confidentiality and privacy is necessary to provide a safe place where people can feel comfortable enough to be open and honest about their experience and to request guidance without fearing negative ramifications in their careers or any area of their lives.

Holistic View

This way of recovery isn't limited only to interior awareness (i.e., finding freedom from identification with one's thoughts and emotions). That's an important aspect of it, but those participating are encouraged to take a more holistic view of their recovery.

A holistic view does more than emphasize interior awareness. It also respects the physical body, which is why we encourage physical exercise, good nutrition and any other measures that benefit our well-being.

We also encourage people to tend to relationships, family, community, and others within the Natural Rest group itself. Shadow work, perspective taking, and the Boomerang Inquiry are three aspects of this way of recovery that deal with relationship issues. These practices, when coupled with presence, bring a natural harmony to our relationships. As peace and well-being are realized within, this is reflected in all areas of our lives.

Natural Rest Isn't a Substitute for Rehab

If you're currently using alcohol, drugs, or other chemicals, we strongly encourage you to seek professional help if you cannot quit on your own. This way of recovery is *not* a substitute for medical attention and it's *not* a detoxification program. Detoxification under the supervision of health care professionals may be necessary before you begin the Natural Rest way. You should always consult a physician, health care, or addiction specialist before and during your participation in this or any other program.

The practices and inquiries in this book are also not a substitute for some other treatment or recovery program or method that's working positively for you. This way of recovery can powerfully complement what you already have. We ask you to ease into the practices and inquiries here to see if they work for you, before abandoning other methods or recovery programs that have been helpful. For those who are ready, natural rest can be the key to complete freedom from the addictive cycle.

A Word to the Reader

This book contains many short paragraphs separated by spaces. These short paragraphs are invitations for you to deeply experience the words themselves and to look into your own direct experience of the restful presence to which the words point.

Take a moment of rest between each paragraph.

You're invited to read this book as an ongoing invitation to relax into the natural rest of this moment. If this book helps you, keep it nearby so you can refer to it as a reminder to rest in presence.

This book is not about the intellect. The intellect is a tool available to us. We continue using the intellect in our lives. But the wisdom and clarity available in natural rest comes from a deeper source. This wisdom and clarity is available to all humans through experientially resting in presence as often as possible.

Although many insights can arise in the mind through resting in presence, the clarity of natural rest doesn't come from agreeing or disagreeing with whatever's said here. If you find yourself arguing with the words of this book, it's probably coming from the frustration of not seeing where the words are pointing. Seek support from someone who has direct experience with finding recovery through natural rest.

One way you may find yourself arguing with the words in this book is by feeling frustrated with the sheer repetition of some of the main instructions (e.g., the instruction to "rest" or "allow all en-

ergies to be as they are"). If you find yourself frustrated in this way, it may be that you are trying to read the book to feed the intellect, looking for more information on each page or reading the book as if it is a story unfolding before you eyes. This book in not designed to fill your mind with more ideas, tell a story, or even to provide complicated theories of addiction to learn or memorize. The repetition of these instructions is deliberately placed in the book as a constant reminder to experience presence for yourself. This is why taking time between paragraphs to rest and look to where the words are pointing is so vital. Avoid reading the book from beginning to end, as you would read other books. Instead, just read a little bit every morning, evening, or throughout the day, taking time in between to rest and experience the freedom to which the words are pointing.

Natural rest is different than other recovery programs. It's an unlearning, revealing that life is a mystery that can never be fully understood. It can only be lived. In this recognition, we rely less on thoughts for our well-being. We come to know our well-being in presence instead.

Some will not be attracted to this way of recovery. They may be more interested in continuing to seek the future. This book remains available if that search ever becomes exhausting.

The Structure of This Book

"Chapter One: Natural Rest" is a basic guide for experiencing presence on a repeated basis throughout each day. It may be helpful to return to this chapter regularly as a reminder that nothing stands in the way of resting in presence in any moment.

Presence is always available, no matter where you are, no matter what's happening.

When you first start this way of recovery, keeping the attitude that presence is always available is helpful. This open attitude empowers you. It helps you put to rest any notion that your well-being is somehow only available at certain times of the day or that it's dependent on what happens to you or on outside sources.

The source of your well-being is presence itself, which is never dependent on any of these things. The present moment is always here. It contains the well-being you've been seeking.

In your quest for the next moment, you've been overlooking this treasure all of your life.

The other chapters deal with topics such as cravings, obsession, self-centeredness, seeking energy, relationships, stories of self-deficiency, Natural Rest groups, misconceptions and traps, and selflessness.

If, before beginning the practice of repeatedly resting in presence, you want to learn more about the mental and emotional structure within you that has kept you trapped in the addictive cycle, read "Chapter Four: Self-Centeredness" before anything else. Chapter

Four can be helpful in understanding the structure and nature of addictive seeking and why presence is so important.

"Chapter Seven: The Living Inquiries" introduces and explains the Compulsion Inquiry and the other Living Inquiries, which are important components of this way of recovery.

"Chapter Eight: Natural Rest Groups" is a guide to both forming a group and conducting meetings.

The final chapter, "Selflessness," is an explanation of the benefits of this way of recovery. Through natural rest, self-centered addiction is transformed into selfless presence.

Presence as a Way to Recover

Before you dig into this book, it's important to explain a little about the context. In this book, natural rest is referred to as a "way of recovery" for a reason. Seeking toward the future is one of the hallmarks of addiction. A recovery program that has us chasing the future has at least the possibility of feeding the addictive cycle within us.

If the key to freedom from addiction is found through presence, then how can presence be reached via a way? Doesn't the word "way" itself imply a time-bound method—that is, the movement from now to some point in the future?

To answer that, we have to take a closer look at who we are as humans. We're used to thinking of ourselves as stories involving a past, present, and future. All our lives, we've been conditioned to think of the future as the key to unlocking whatever it is we're seeking. So at first, it's only natural that we approach this way of recovery within that same, familiar way of thinking.

Yet, through the Natural Rest way, we eventually wake up and out of this conditioning—out of the false belief that we must somehow seek the future to find our sense of fulfillment or well-being. As we rest in presence, we come to see that we're already whole and complete in the here and now. We find less need to identify with thoughts of the past and future. As this happens, our stories become less important to us. And, as our stories become less important, our sense of living in time gradually dissolves, leaving only the peace and freedom of timeless presence.

Some may begin to practice this way and discover instantaneous presence. They're ready to live there! Because it happened so quickly, they might not experience resting in presence as a way or method at all.

For most of us, however, a complete recognition of presence doesn't happen in one fleeting instant or even overnight. For that reason, this book was created as a way to ease you into restful presence, gradually. Although this may give the impression that you're moving toward the realization of presence in the future, in actuality, the story of needing the future is falling away.

How long does it take for you to recognize presence in all areas of your life? It will take exactly how long it takes. So relax and enjoy the ride! And always, always, always . . . trust your own experience.

CHAPTER ONE: Natural Rest

The Practice

This book is an ongoing invitation to relax repeatedly in thought-free presence. Taking brief moments of thought-free rest, repeatedly, throughout the day is the central practice here.

We make a decision to relax into the present moment just as it is, completely and without reservation.

We do this throughout the day, repeatedly. "Repeatedly" means as often as possible. Make the practice of taking brief moments of rest your number one priority throughout the day.

What is natural rest? Don't try to think about it. Relax for three to five seconds right now and simply be *without any conceptual labels* for what's presently happening.

Stop thinking for one moment! Right now!

Relax your body and mind. Take a deep breath if you have to.

Notice that you have the capacity to be aware of thought. Notice the thought that's currently happening. Look directly at that thought and watch it fade away. As it fades, simply rest as the thought-free space. For a few seconds add no additional thoughts. This is a brief moment of rest.

What's here, in this moment, when you aren't labeling it? Nothing can be said. Nothing needs to be known. For a few seconds, past and future thoughts aren't arising. Addictive seeking arises through emphasizing past and future thoughts. So when you're taking a brief moment of rest, you're already completely free of the story of past and future. You're already presently free of addictive seeking in this moment.

Stop thinking for brief moments! *Just be, without thought, for three to five seconds, repeatedly, throughout the day.*

Does it take a thought to just be? No, so just be! This is the natural rest.

Notice there's a simple, restful awareness here in the present moment. It's the same awareness that's been here all of our lives. (Please note that the words "presence" and "awareness" are used synonymously throughout this book.)

Different energies, such as thoughts, emotions, cravings, obsessions, states, sensations, and experiences, come and go within awareness, but awareness is always here. Without this awareness, nothing can be experienced.

Awareness isn't any thought, emotion, craving, obsession, state, experience, sight, sound, smell, taste, or other sensation that appears and disappears. It's not any of these things. These things are all temporary.

Different stories have come and gone within this presence throughout our lives. The story coming through when we were ten years old is different than the story coming through at age twenty, thirty, and so on. But the presence in which those stories come and go *never* changes.

It's the same presence, no matter what's coming through.

In taking brief moments of resting in presence, we come to see for ourselves that this is the same presence. This provides a stability and well-being in our lives that temporary stories and other energies cannot provide.

Presence is *that which is aware of* all of these temporary energies coming and going.

If, at first, we find it difficult to rest in presence, we may start by noticing only a subtle sense of presence in the chest. It may be just a felt-sense of peace within that you notice in the very moment you stop thinking.

Presence is like pure space. There's always a sense of being *here* in the silent, still space of the present moment. All we have to do is *notice this space and rest as the space.*

Start by sensing the *space* within the body. Then notice the *space* outside the body. Notice it everywhere.

Rest into the silent, still space repeatedly, throughout the day.

As we repeatedly bring attention to this felt-sense of presence in the chest, the body, and in the space of the present moment, this presence becomes more and more prominent.

It becomes easier to rest naturally in the present moment, anchoring awareness again and again in the space of the inner body and also in the larger space of the present moment outside the body.

When we stop emphasizing thoughts and make resting in presence the most important thing in our lives, we come to see this inner body space and outer body space as one undivided space. This space is the natural rest.

Each time we rest throughout the day, we experience the relaxed, open view of the present moment. Instead of narrowly focusing on a story in the mind or a single object, person or event, we take in the fullness of the present moment without thought and allow our focus to be wide open and relaxed. We notice space in front of, behind, between and all around everything we see. As we take a brief moment without thought, the present moment is experienced as one, undivided tapestry of space, sensations, emotions, colors, shapes, sounds, smells and tastes. Relaxing into this open view is very beneficial. It helps reduce stress, anxiety and addictive thinking.

Only thoughts create a sense of division.

In this natural rest, we allow all sights, sounds, smells, and other sensations to be noticed more. Life starts to feel more alive as we stop emphasizing thoughts for brief moments throughout the day and start being aware of these present sensations without labeling them.

Presence is the space in which life actually happens. Our thoughts are coming and going within the space of the present moment, and these thoughts are merely telling a self-centered story.

This story has been trying to escape the present moment. It's a time-bound story. In the story, we're always rehashing the past and fantasizing about a better future. We continuously overlook this moment, where life *actually* happens.

As we rest in presence more and more, this moment stops feeling like a fleeting instant or a quick flash between the past and future. We begin to experience the present moment as the stable, unchanging, open, clear, undivided space in which all energies come and go.

Energies include thoughts. We come to see that the story of who we are is a set of thoughts based on the past and future. Each of these thoughts temporarily appears and disappears in the unchanging, stable space of the present moment.

Our stories are constantly changing. When we emphasize thoughts instead of resting in presence, the temporary nature of thought leaves us feeling unstable about whom we are. This makes us seek the future to find a sense of self. Yet, we never find a complete version of ourselves this way. We only find more seeking toward the future.

Look now and notice that the story of who you think you are appears through thoughts. Notice that thoughts are always either words or mental pictures. Take one moment and just allow all words and mental pictures to come to rest. In that moment, there's nothing to seek.

Seeing that our story is made only of this stream of words and pictures, and that each word and picture is temporary and unstable, allows us to trust the natural rest of presence completely. Presence provides a mental and emotional stability that's not available in our stories. It's the key to freedom from the addictive cycle of constantly seeking the future.

Be still as often as possible throughout the day.

Notice the stillness within the body and mind.

Notice that silence is everywhere, under the noise of life.

Notice the present space where life happens.

Stillness, silence, and space are doorways into the natural rest of this moment. In this way of recovery, we let ourselves sink completely into the still, silent space of the present moment as often as possible. *This is the key.*

Resting becomes easier and more natural the more we do it. The moments get longer and longer. Through this practice, we come to realize presence as our real identity. The story of the seeker who can't get enough is allowed to dissolve completely into the fullness of the present moment.

There's Nothing to Chase

In addiction, we live with a story of deficiency, a sense of needing something else, something more in the future. It always feels like something is missing in life. This story of deficiency is a set of words that repeatedly say, "I'm not good enough," "I'm not there yet," or "There's something wrong with me." This story arises with painful emotions and/or sensations of restlessness or boredom.

In order to escape these feelings and sensations, we unconsciously emphasize thoughts about the future. Thoughts arise that tell us we need to seek a pleasurable high in the next moment in order to cover up boredom, restlessness, or painful feelings that we're experiencing in the body.

When we emphasize these thoughts, instead of resting in presence, they lead us into the cycle of seeking the future. We never find permanent relief this way. We only find a temporary fix, which leads us to chase the pleasurable high, again and again.

A pleasurable high is only temporary. The story of deficiency and its corresponding emotions and sensations return once the high wears off, leading us back into the cycle of seeking a fix in the next moment.

We're like dogs chasing our own tails.

Restful presence is experienced to be complete just as it is. Resting in brief moments of thought-free presence repeatedly throughout the day frees us from this endless chase.

The Equality of Energies

Emphasizing certain energies causes us to suffer and seek the future for release from the suffering.

Energies include anything that's not at rest or anything that comes and goes within stable, restful presence including thoughts, emotions, states, sensations, experiences, cravings, anxiety, obsessions, or seeking.

In the addictive cycle, our way of coping with life has been to distract ourselves from uncomfortable or painful thoughts and emotions, cover them up in some way, or seek some future moment of release.

In this cycle, we're avoiding negative thoughts and feelings and emphasizing or seeking positive thoughts and feelings.

This is the very definition of seeking—to push away or cover up what's actually appearing in favor of looking for something else that we think should be appearing.

We have been emphasizing certain stories from the past, making them more important than the present moment. We rehash certain painful situations that have happened to us. It may be an old relationship, a trauma, the loss of a job, or even a recent, painful argument with a loved one.

Nothing ever really gets resolved this way. In constantly replaying these stories, we keep them alive. We carry them through time, emphasizing them over the simple, natural rest of presence. We stay locked in a self-centered story.

We've also been emphasizing fearful thoughts and emotions. We play out fearful scenarios about future events that may threaten us. Nothing ever really gets resolved this way either. We just stay locked in the story, taking action from fear rather than from the wisdom of presence.

We often don't see that we're doing all of this.

Most of the time, this constant movement of emphasizing certain energies over others is unconscious. If we could fully see that we're causing our own suffering and seeking and had the power to stop it, we'd stop immediately.

But we don't see it. So we just keep seeking relief in the future. In this way of recovery, our commitment is to rest in presence repeatedly, whenever possible. We no longer make temporary energies more important than resting in presence. This provides the well-being we've been seeking.

Through resting in presence, it becomes easier to see what's happening. This habit of emphasizing certain energies is brought into the light of present awareness.

Emphasizing certain energies creates a mental and emotional imbalance and instability in our lives. This imbalance and instability naturally leads us to seek the future and to look for substances and activities that will make us feel better.

In restful presence, we stop replaying the past and being afraid of the future. We stop trying to avoid uncomfortable or painful thoughts and feelings carried over from the past. We stop trying to seek the future for release from the pain and discomfort.

All of this happens automatically through the practice of making restful presence the most important thing in our lives.

Through resting in presence, we begin to experience these energies as a fluid and natural flow. No thought is emphasized over any other thought. No state or experience is emphasized over any other. We come to see that no energy movement has the power to destroy the stability of presence. We see that all energies are equal, regardless of their content. All energies arise, hang around awhile, and then disappear, leaving no trace. Presence remains stable through the arising and falling of all energies.

Resting in presence throughout the day provides an unshakable peace in our lives.

Energies Are Allowed to Be Exactly as They Are

Each energy movement appears within the spacious rest of presence and then disappears. In each disappearance, the rest is realized again and again. In this rest, the need to chase after or do something with the next energy movement relaxes.

These energies are inescapable movements of the rest itself. By relaxing repeatedly into the natural rest of presence, we see these energies come and go. We face these energies directly for the first time.

Resting in presence automatically and effortlessly provides the stability to allow life to be as it is.

Resting allows all energies to be as they are. We simply notice them come and go without needing to add to, subtract from, change, or get rid of any of them.

To notice a thought, emotion, or other energy movement means to watch it appear and then disappear. It means to not dwell on it in any manner. To see it is to notice its temporary nature, and to let it pass without trying to add to or subtract anything from it.

We're no longer running away from this moment into the future. In no longer escaping, each energy movement is allowed to be exactly as it is. There's no need to modify, alter, neutralize, or get rid of any energy movement.

Each time we move to modify, alter, neutralize, or try to get rid of the energies arising, we're back in the cycle of addictive seeking. We're looking for something else, something more. We're trying to control our experience and the thoughts and feelings coming through. We're overlooking the natural rest of presence.

This Isn't About the Future

Resting in presence is not an ego-based future achievement. We take it easy on ourselves. We choose to make natural rest the most important thing, in the here and now.

The here and now is where life is.

We ease into our decision by repeatedly relaxing into the present moment throughout the day. We don't look for quick results. We don't look for future results. We simply rest in the thought-free space of the present moment. We come to realize that restful presence is our home, our freedom from the addictive cycle.

We sink deeper and deeper into presence, falling more and more in love with whatever's appearing right now.

No More Escaping Emotions and Sensations

We sometimes experience sadness, loneliness, grief, anger, or resentment in conjunction with thoughts about the past. Other times, we experience frustration, stress, or anger in conjunction with thoughts about challenging situations that are happening in the present moment. Whenever we emphasize thoughts about the future, we experience anxiety and fear.

When these emotions or sensations arise, we simply notice whatever thoughts are appearing. We let those thoughts come to rest. We bring attention into the space of the inner body. We don't label whatever emotion is appearing in the body. We just let the emotion be exactly as it is, within that space.

Letting this energy be as it is allows it to effortlessly change itself into presence. We don't do the changing through effort. It happens all on its own, simply because we choose to rest in awareness.

All emotions are like clouds of smoke. They dissipate on their own. We don't have to push them away, suppress, or manipulate them. All we have to do is notice the space in which the emotion is appearing and then let the energy of the emotion dissipate naturally in the same way a cloud of smoke dissipates on its own.

If the intensity of thought starts up again, we take another moment to *feel* the energy directly in the body without mentally labeling it. This practice has enormous benefits in that it releases the emotional energy driving our mental suffering.

For the first time in our lives, we're not trying to mentally escape our feelings. They're faced directly. What does it mean to face an emotion? It means *to allow the energy of the emotion to be as it is, without placing words, pictures, or labels on it.* We don't even call an energy "fear," "sadness," "bad," or "good." Those are labels. We rest in thought-free presence, letting the raw energy of the emotion come through without any story attached to it. We do the same with any uncomfortable sensations like tightness, resistance, or physical pain. This becomes easier the more we rest in presence, repeatedly, throughout the day. In restful, thought-free presence, we're not emphasizing the self-centered story that has been trying to escape painful feelings and uncomfortable sensations.

In these brief moments, the movement to escape can relax.

Escaping is the tendency to move into the future, away from unpleasant present energies and toward pleasant future energies. All escaping happens through emphasizing words and pictures in the story.

By relaxing repeatedly into restful, present awareness, we see that escape is no longer needed. Resting in presence and noticing that all energies naturally come and go within presence is all that's needed.

The transformation available here doesn't come through determination and effort. Presence does all the work. The only thing we have to do is make the choice to *relax* into the present moment on a repeated basis and let all energies come and go uninterrupted.

Natural Rest Is Our Home

We take brief moments in which we allow all thoughts to relax into the peaceful space of the present moment. We find our home in this rest.

What do we mean when we say "presence is our home"? This "home" is not something we find, like an object, a place, a state, or even a single experience. It is not a thought either. It is the recognition that all energies come and go, and what remains cannot be understood. It cannot be grasped. It is peace itself. We call it "home" because, as we rest more and more, this rest feels natural and available always. All of these words are merely ways to describe the experiential seeing that no matter what energies are coming through, they simply pass once we notice them and not follow them. Presence is freedom from believing we are our thoughts and the other temporary energies that come and go.

Nothing that comes and goes temporarily can be what we really are.

As we notice the rest of the present moment as always available, life is experienced as peaceful, free, open, and uncontrived. We find less or no need to apply effort to mentally label or control our experience, others, the world, or ourselves. We are naturally open to any thoughts, emotions, or other energies that may appear and then disappear.

We see that these thoughts have no power to destroy or divide the natural rest of presence. They're temporary energies. That's all.

In the natural rest of presence, we're not at war with thoughts. We don't need to be. They have their place. In fact, we continue to use thinking for practical purposes such as driving a car, talking to a friend, working, or buying groceries. Resting in thought-free presence means resting in this moment without our *personal* stories. Practical thoughts are still useful. It's the rest from our personal stories that provides the key to freedom from addiction.

In the beginning, we may experience rest as a temporary state that we visit repeatedly throughout the day. But through repeatedly relaxing into the natural rest of the present moment, we come to see rest not as a temporary state, but as the very nature of our being.

Don't take the words "natural rest" on as a belief. Rest is an energetic relaxation into the present moment, as it is. This relaxation is essential to our well-being as a whole. It is felt and experienced in your whole being, body, mind, and all around you.

Natural Rest Is Always Available

We come to experience natural rest as available always in the here and now. It's available whether we're still or moving. It's available equally when things are going well in our lives or when they're not going well. It's available in moments of excessive thinking or in moments of not thinking at all.

It's available in calm moments and stressful moments, in moments of peace, and moments of extreme obsession or conflict, when alone, or in the company of others.

All it takes is the decision to rest in presence. This opportunity is always available.

We relax into the spaciousness and peacefulness of the present moment, whenever possible, throughout the day, no matter what's happening. Spacious, restful awareness is always here. All we have to do is relax into this rest and see that the only thing obscuring it is the movement to emphasize energies coming through.

Once we start to see what these energies are, we can easily spot them whenever they arise. We can let them come and go without trying to do anything with them.

In recognizing rest as the very nature of our being, it's allowed to permeate every aspect of our lives, every experience, and all energies that come and go. This is why we call it "natural." It begins to no longer feel like a decision we're making or a practice we're employing. It's simply available, always, as our real identity.

This must be experienced. It cannot be grasped through thinking.

This Isn't About Ending Thought

Recognizing the natural rest of presence doesn't mean we no longer think. It's not about trying to suppress thought permanently. We aren't even trying to be without thought for long periods of time. Remember, simply take brief moments of rest, three to five seconds at a time, repeatedly throughout the day.

In seeing that each thought is temporary, we become interested in the presence in which thought happens. We stop emphasizing thoughts for a sense of self as they come through. We know that emphasizing thoughts has never brought us the freedom we so desperately seek as addicts. Emphasizing thoughts causes suffering and seeking.

We don't force ourselves into presence. We simply relax the body and mind completely, whenever possible. We let whatever thought is appearing to gently come to rest. As a thought comes to rest, we notice the thought-free space that's already present. We notice this space and we trust it completely. In this way, we're not at war with the words and pictures that arise in the thought stream. We simply see them as temporary energies coming and going within a more stable, restful presence. We rely on presence rather than emphasizing the temporary words and pictures.

By resting in that space as often as possible throughout the day, we naturally begin to identify with thought less and less. We find a sweet and peaceful presence at the core of our being.

We're finally home. We don't have to seek anymore. We're at rest.

The Pond Metaphor

Imagine a pond in your mind's eye. The pond is completely still on a summer day. It's totally at rest in its natural state.

Like the pond, the natural rest of presence is quiet and still.

Like ripples across the surface of the pond, words, pictures and bodily energies appear and disappear within quiet, still, restful presence.

Rather than recognizing the natural restfulness of presence (the pond), we've been looking for a permanent sense of self where it can't be found (in the ever-changing temporary ripples).

The temporary energies coming through have been taking up all of our attention. We've been emphasizing these energies, chasing the pleasure and avoiding the pain. This keeps us constantly seeking.

We've been operating on the assumption that seeking is necessary. We've been assuming that it takes thought to simply live and be. We've been assuming that it takes worry, anxiety, and stress in order to live.

None of these things are essential to life. Presence is the only thing that's essential because presence is always here. Resting and relaxing in present awareness throughout the day is the simplest, most effective thing we can do for ourselves as addicts.

The simple practice of resting in presence reveals that seeking, worrying, and excessive thinking aren't necessary at all. Restful presence is already free of everything.

Just as each ripple across the pond is inseparable from the pond itself, we see that each energy movement is inseparable from the rest.

This inseparability is important in seeing that each ripple is a movement of the pond itself. In this seeing, we don't try to push any ripple away. We aren't trying to get rid of the energies that move through our restful presence.

All energies are allowed.

No ripple is closer or more essential to the pond than any other ripple. Each ripple is equally wet and equally "of the pond." The pond is always there, no matter what ripple is moving across its surface.

Similarly, no thought, emotion, or other energy movement is closer or more essential to presence than any other movement. Each is an equal movement of presence. Presence is always here, no matter what's moving through. Coming to know this through direct experience has incredible transformative power.

Keep It Simple

In this chapter and throughout the remainder of the book, the word "energies" is used to describe the coming and going of appearances within presence. In this chapter, we've described energies as thoughts, emotions, cravings, obsessions, fixations, anxiety, seeking, sensations, states and experiences. That's a long list. It may be helpful to keep it much simpler than that. Energies are really just three things: words, pictures and bodily energy.

When you see the word "thoughts" in this book, notice in your own experience that thoughts are always either words or pictures. "I really want some wine" are words. The image of wine that appears in your mind is a picture. These words and pictures are movements of energy taking certain forms in your experience. That's all they are. The sensation you feel in your body is the bodily energy. It doesn't matter whether you think that energy is an emotion or sensation. When you don't label it with words, it is experienced as energy coming and going. It just happens to be taking the form of something felt in the body, rather than as words or pictures.

Resting in presence refers to noticing words, pictures, and bodily energy coming and going. For brief moments throughout the day, let all words and pictures come to rest so that bodily energy is allowed to be as it is, without putting words or pictures on it. Without words or pictures, the energy more easily moves and dissolves. Keeping it this simple, by breaking down your experience to words, pictures and bodily energy, makes resting easier. Your mind is less involved in describing what you are experiencing as anxiety, obsession or something else.

Notice that, when you feel compelled to reach for your favorite addictive substance or activity, you aren't resting and noticing words and pictures come and go. You are believing them or following them. And you are not aware directly of bodily energy. Addiction is essentially the experience of words and/or pictures feeling stuck to bodily energy. That's what creates the compulsive desire to reach for your favorite substance or activity. You are thinking instead of resting and noticing. Addiction continues only when we are "in our heads" in this way, not feeling bodily energy directly and letting it come to rest on its own. Resting and being aware of words, pictures and bodily energy helps you keep from following every urge or desire that arises. It helps the urge or desire to relax. This will become even clearer when you begin to use the Compulsion Inquiry and the other Living Inquiries, discussed later in the book.

Key Points

Rest in Thought-Free Presence Repeatedly Throughout the Day. Throughout the day, as often as possible, relax into the present moment without emphasizing thoughts (i.e., words and mental pictures). Remember: just three to five seconds at a time.

Rest Even While Words and Pictures Are Appearing. Even when words and pictures are appearing, you can rest as the awareness that notices them coming and going. While resting in a relaxed, open way, the words and pictures can be allowed to be as they are, without trying to add to, subtract from, or change the words and pictures in any way. Every now and then, whenever you think of it, let all words and pictures come to rest just by watching them dissolve in awareness as stated in the first key point. This helps you feel bodily energy directly, as stated in the next key point.

Let All Bodily Energies Be As They Are. Let all bodily energies come and go freely and equally without emphasizing or analyzing them. Let them be as they are. Don't place words or mental pictures on them. This allows bodily energies to change or dissolve more easily. It helps keep us from reaching for addictive substances and activities to medicate, cover up, suppress or change how we feel.

CHAPTER TWO Cravings

Notice Cravings as Soon as They Arise

Cravings are energies that come and go temporarily within restful presence. Nothing more! Because of their temporary nature, they initially have no power to harm us. They only gain power when they arise—unseen. To say that a craving arises unseen means we don't see it as a temporary thought that carries with it a corresponding sensation in the body. Whenever we notice that a craving is only a thought with a sensation, it becomes easier to relax in presence, and allow the thought and sensation to arise and fall naturally.

Sometimes cravings arise as thoughts such as, "I'd really like a beer."

But they *don't* always rise to the level of thought. In fact, they often start at a level prior to thought—as subtle movements of energy in the body—like tiny sensations in the stomach or chest.

Imagine a soapy bubble rising out of a hot bath. This is how cravings appear . . . subtly. They're small movements of anxious energy that arise from the restful space within the body.

Whenever we fail to notice these sensations the moment they appear in the body or soon after, they can gain power and momentum. They often fuel a rapid firing of thoughts related to substances or activities we crave (e.g., gambling, sweets, a drug of choice).

In other words, they turn from mild cravings into obsession.

Regardless of whether a craving first arises as a thought or sensation in the body, the invitation is always the same: relax into presence and simply notice these energies as they come and go within presence—without emphasizing them.

If a craving arises as a thought, just notice the thought, then let it pass. If necessary, take a deeeeeeeeep breath and then relax. For a moment, just be without any thought. That's the *natural rest.*

Witness each thought come and go without emphasizing it; then bring your attention straight into the space of the inner body. Notice any sensations in the body, like a subtle movement of energy in the chest or stomach area.

This bodily energy is the fuel behind all thought-based cravings.

To notice a craving energy arising in the body doesn't mean to label it. Don't call it "good" or "bad" or even "a craving." There's nothing to mentally analyze or rationalize about the energy.

To notice a craving means to recognize the space around the raw energy arising and then to bring your attention right into the middle of the energy and rest it there, without words or pictures on it. This allows it to pass more easily and naturally on its own.

Subtle cravings gain momentum when we don't let the sensation arise and fall freely without labels. The thought, "I want a beer" can feel stuck to the sensation that's arising in the body. This experience of thoughts being stuck to sensations is called the "Velcro Effect."

Resting and feeling into the sensation without words and pictures on it undoes the Velcro Effect.

If the word "craving" or any other thought or word appears, we simply allow it to come and go just as we'd notice a bird flying past us. When a bird flies by, we don't try to grasp it. We merely let it fly. We see its flight as a temporary arising.

Each thought is like a bird, a temporary arising.

We allow each arising thought that comments on a craving to simply come and go without emphasizing the thought. Remember, thoughts are always words or pictures. Whenever you see words or mental pictures about your favorite substance or activity, let those words or pictures come to rest by observing them directly. For a few seconds add no other words or pictures. Rest for a few seconds in thought-free presence and let the raw energy of sensation in the body come and go.

Whenever we experience a craving energy in the body, all sorts of thoughts can arise, including thoughts about wanting to use our favorite drug and thoughts about wanting the craving to go away.

But it doesn't matter what thought arises, just let it pass. Don't emphasize it. Even the thought, "I want this to go away," can subtly keep the sensation around. Relax without that thought, too.

Each time a thought comes and goes, take a moment to rest in presence. Then again, bring your attention to the space of the inner body.

In noticing the craving as an energy movement in the body, we can allow it to be exactly as it is. Revisit the cloud of smoke metaphor from *Chapter One.* A cloud of smoke has its own short life span. If we don't try to manipulate it in any way, it eventually dissipates into thin air completely on its own. It's the same with an inner body craving; it also has its own short life span. If we don't emphasize any thoughts about it, it simply dissipates into pure presence completely on its own.

If we experience any resistance within the body to the arising and falling of the craving, we simply notice the resistance. In noticing the resistant energy, it's also allowed to simply be. It relaxes into presence once we stop labeling it "resistance."

By noticing a craving energy in the body and letting it come and go without emphasizing any thoughts about it, the craving loses its capacity to fuel obsessive thoughts.

Don't Wait For Cravings to Appear

Throughout the day, it's important to relax repeatedly into the natural rest of the present moment, instead of waiting for a craving to appear. Rest in moments even when no cravings arise.

In this way of recovery, we don't think of resting as a "remedy for cravings." Natural rest isn't another "fix." In our addictive cycle, we're always looking for the next quick fix.

In the natural rest way, we don't treat recovery as a fix.

Cravings arise and fall in presence. That's all they do. They come and they go, leaving no trace. They have no other power.

In spacious, present awareness, we're better able to notice cravings as soon as they arise within the body, *before* they begin fueling addictive and obsessive thoughts about the future.

When we treat presence as a quick fix, we're back in the addictive cycle, looking for temporary relief. When we treat resting in presence as a shift in our identity, we free ourselves from the addictive cycle, permanently. For more on this identity shift, see *Chapter Four: Self-Centeredness.*

Key Points

Notice Thought-Cravings. Sometimes cravings first appear as thoughts and are accompanied by sensations or energy movements in the chest or stomach area. It can seem as if the thoughts are stuck to the sensations. This is the Velcro Effect.

Thoughts are always words or pictures. For example, "I want a beer" is a set of words. An image of a beer can and the image of driving to the store to buy beer are both pictures. Notice the moment that words or pictures arise about wanting to use or engage in an addictive substance or activity. In noticing the thought, let the thought come to rest. For a few seconds add no thoughts. Rest in thought-free presence. Bring your attention into the space of the inner body. Let the energy movement in the body be exactly as it is without emphasizing any labels about it. Let it dissipate completely on its own. This undoes the Velcro Effect.

Notice Body-Cravings. Cravings don't always arise initially as thoughts. They often arise as sensations in the chest or stomach area, small energy movements that propel you toward an addictive substance or activity.

Notice the moment a sensation of craving appears within the body. Noticing this energy the moment it appears is an opportunity to relax into restful presence.

Bring your attention directly into the bodily energy, without placing any words or pictures on it. Let it be exactly as it is. Notice the space around the energy also. Notice how the energy just hangs in the space. Let it hang there for however long it needs to. Let it dissolve naturally on its own. If, while resting with the sensation, you see words or pictures arise, just notice them and watch them directly until they come to rest. Then bring attention right back into the energy and let it be until it dissolves. Watching words and pictures come to rest and bringing attention back to the energy by itself undoes the Velcro Effect. This releases the desire for the substance or activity.

As you are taking brief moments of thought-free rest throughout the day, it becomes easier to notice that thought-cravings and body-cravings come and go within that rest.

CHAPTER THREE
Obsession

A Definition of Obsession

In *Chapter Two,* we discussed cravings. In this chapter, our focus is obsession. These are related energies. Think of obsession as a very intense craving energy that seems to overtake the body and mind in an unconscious way.

You can even think of cravings and obsessions as existing on a continuum. Cravings can appear in increasing intensity from mild to moderate until they cross a certain threshold of intensity. At that point, they're obsessions.

Obsessions often lead to compulsive, addictive "acting out" behavior and even relapse.

Let's start with a basic definition of obsession. For purposes of this book, we define obsession as *"persistent, intense, unconscious energy in the body accompanied by a continuous, involuntary preoccupation with thought that cannot be removed by logic or reasoning."*

That's a wordy definition. But it's important to speak to all of the elements of obsession so that we know what's happening to us in those moments of obsession, why our old ways of dealing with obsession haven't totally worked, and how restful presence frees this obsessive energy.

Breaking Down the Definition

Persistent, intense, and unconscious

Obsession has a persistent intensity to it that rises above mild to moderate cravings. Obsession is like being completely overtaken by intense mental and emotional energy.

Obsession is a raging storm within the body and mind with its own self-sustaining power and momentum. It seems to be driven toward a purpose, which is to escape into an addictive substance or activity. It's seeking the future.

"Unconsciousness" is similar to the notion of "seeing red" when one is angry. If you ask someone after a moment of intense anger to relate what actually happened in that moment, he or she isn't likely able to describe clearly what happened within his or her mind and body. The anger was unconscious in that moment, which means it was unseen. In the moment it arose, there was no awareness of the anger.

Similarly, in obsessive moments, whenever they first appear, both the thoughts and the bodily energies are not seen by awareness. This unconsciousness is the fuel for obsession. It's like a small spark that starts a massive fire. When the spark remains unseen, it grows and grows. Obsession can only continue as long as the thoughts and energies remain unseen. We'll talk more about this later.

Energy in the body

Obsession isn't just thought-based. Our bodies are very active in moments of obsession. Heat, tension, vibration, anxiety, fear, and other energies rise up in the body whenever we're obsessing about our addictive substance or activity. Our throats may close. Our chests may tighten. Our stomachs may clinch.

Without knowing what's actually happening within our bodies, we tend to oversimplify obsession, believing it's just a "thought problem." Remember, it's the Velcro Effect that lies at the heart of addiction. Thoughts arise and feel stuck to these sensations of heat, tension, vibration, anxiety, fear, and other energies in the body.

The key to releasing obsession is found through resting in presence, so that the Velcro Effect is undone.

By treating it only as a thought problem, we erroneously believe we can appeal to logic and reasoning (more thoughts) to free ourselves from obsession. This is a vicious, nonproductive cycle where the thought-based personal will is only trying to overcome itself. This cycle ignores what's really happening within the body.

Continuous, involuntary preoccupation with thought that cannot be removed by logic or reasoning

There's certainly a strong element of thought in obsession and the thought feels involuntary as if we're at its mercy.

This preoccupation with thought cannot be removed by logic or reasoning.

It's difficult, if not impossible, to think our way out of obsession. It's like being caught in a raging storm and then believing we can reason with the storm and tell it to calm down. The futility of this becomes more apparent as we begin to relax repeatedly into the natural rest of the present moment.

Freedom from Obsession

It's important to not wait until cravings reach the point of obsession. Remember, the invitation here is to relax repeatedly, throughout the day, as restful presence. Don't think of presence as a remedy, a fix, or an antidote that you apply only when full-blown obsession is happening.

Despite the fact that this chapter will give you a plan for dealing with moments of obsession (see Stop, Notice, Rest, Repeat or SNoRRe below), we want to rest in presence throughout the day, not just when obsession is happening.

In *Chapter One,* we said: *In the beginning, we may experience rest as a temporary state that we visit repeatedly throughout the day. But through repeatedly relaxing into the natural rest of the present moment, we come to see rest not as a temporary state, but as the very nature of our being.*

Repeatedly relaxing into present rest reveals a natural well-being, available always in the here and now. Rest isn't a quick fix for the problem of obsession. That kind of thinking may lead us to refuse to rest until the point at which obsession has overtaken us.

Obsession is such a powerful storm that waiting for those moments to practice natural rest often results in frustration. We walk away thinking, "Natural rest didn't help me get rid of my obsession!" This is a misunderstanding of the invitation here.

By relaxing repeatedly throughout the day, in all situations, even pleasant non-obsessive moments, "we come to see rest not as a temporary state, but as the very nature of our being."

This means we rest in *all* situations, whenever we think of it.

By resting repeatedly and by being aware of all energies, including happy thoughts, slight irritations, and mild to moderate cravings (see *Chapter Two: Cravings*) whenever they arise, rest feels more available in intense moments of obsession.

Rest is always available because it's presence itself. Trying to rest for the first time when an obsession has already taken us over is like waiting to walk to the store only after the slight sprinkle of rain outside turns into a downpour. Walk now, whether there's sunshine or a slight sprinkle.

Remember, rest now in whatever situation presents itself! By repeatedly relaxing throughout the day, it becomes easier to rest in presence whenever obsession arises. It can take a while for obsessive energies to completely dissolve and never arise again in your experience.

Stop, Notice, Rest, Repeat (the SNoRRe Method)

If you do find yourself caught in obsession, think of **"stop, notice, rest, and repeat"** or SNoRRe. This is a simple way to explain what it means to rest repeatedly in brief moments of awareness during obsession. The SNoRRe method helps not only with obsession but also with anxiety attacks and other afflictive states.

Short Explanation of the SNoRRe Method

1. **STOP**
   During obsession, take a moment and stop.
2. **NOTICE**
   Notice the current thought. Observe it directly until it disappears. When it comes to rest, quickly bring attention into the body and notice the energy there.
3. **REST**
   With your attention in the body where the energy is, rest without labels for the energy, letting it be exactly as it is. This undoes the Velcro Effect so that the energy in the body can move through naturally without feeling stuck to thoughts.

4. **REPEAT**

   Repeat "stop, notice, and rest" over and over during any obsessive episode.

Long Explanation of the SNoRRe Method

1. **STOP**

   Stop means that, as soon as you recognize obsession happening in the body and mind, stop for one moment. Remember this SNoRRe method.

   Stopping alone is not enough because the mental and emotional energy of obsession often has a tremendous, involuntary force that likes to start again immediately after stopping. This is why it's important to notice, rest, and repeat.

2. **NOTICE**

   Notice includes both noticing thought and noticing bodily energy during obsession.

   Noticing Thought

   As soon as you stop, notice whatever thought is appearing within the mind. This thought is the involuntary preoccupation we talked about in our obsession definition. Noticing the thought makes it conscious or seen. *Remember: unconsciousness is the fuel for obsession.* Simply noticing a thought interrupts it for a brief moment.

   At this point, it's important not to try and think yourself out of obsession. Remember that this preoccupation with thought *cannot be removed by logic or reasoning*. Thinking merely adds more thoughts to a thought stream that's already highly energetic.

Remember that you cannot reason with a storm. Noticing thought is an important opportunity during obsession. For the first time, there's the capacity to see that the awareness that sees the thought is already at rest.

Watch the current thought, whatever it is, until it fades away. Add no additional thoughts for a few seconds.

Noticing Bodily Energy

Noticing thought also provides an even deeper, more important opportunity. It allows you to be aware for the first time of what's happening within your body. People spend years in obsessive behavior without directly recognizing what's actually occurring.

Upon noticing thought, move your attention directly into the body. Notice any heat, tension, vibration, anxiety, fear, or other energies appearing there. There's no need to mentally label, rationalize, or analyze the energies, or why they're there.

Remember, you can't reason with a storm. Just notice the raw energy itself, before the mind labels it. This makes those energies conscious or seen. As long as these energies remain unseen, they fuel obsessive thoughts. Let the energy be as it is, without words or pictures. Experiencing the bodily energy, by itself, without words or pictures undoes the Velcro Effect.

3. **REST**

   Rest means that, once you notice the thought and the bodily energy, rest as awareness. Noticing thought and bodily energies provides the opportunity to rest as the awareness that sees them. Rest means to relax completely into the present moment. Notice the space within your body and within the room. Don't move to apply any force to the thoughts or bodily energies. Let them be exactly as they are.

   This is full acceptance, instead of escape.

   Although thought is often moving energetically and rapidly in the moment of obsession, the awareness that sees the thought is not moving. Awareness is at rest. It simply notices thought. Rest as this awareness that sees thought. Although bodily energy is also very intense, the awareness that sees the bodily energy is not intense. It's at rest. It's simply awake and aware of the energy.

   Awareness is the present, restful awake space in which these thoughts and energies appear.

   Again, we can't reason with a storm. If you find yourself trying to think yourself out of the obsession, let that thought pass. Let each thought pass. Just rest as the awareness that *sees* these thoughts.

   Instead of emphasizing these thoughts, be interested only in the bodily energy. More specifically, notice that the space of the present moment allows the energy to be exactly as it is. Awareness allows bodily energy to be exactly as it is. Experiencing this energy directly without the veil of thought effortlessly converts the energy into presence. Without this bodily energy, obsessive thoughts have no fuel. Obsession dies.

4. **REPEAT**
   Repeat means to repeat "stop, notice, and rest" as often as possible during a strong obsession. Even when you do stop, notice, and rest for a brief moment, obsession often has such a strong pull that it starts right back up. Suddenly, you find yourself taken by the storm once more. Just stop, again. Notice thought and emotion. Rest as awareness. Repeat. Practicing these brief moments over and over during any obsession will allow the energy to withdraw from the obsession itself.

A Practical Example of the SNoRRe Method

Here's an explanation of how the SNoRRe method works in a practical situation:

Imagine you're a gambling addict. You've managed to go a month without gambling. One day, you start having small cravings to gamble.

Having already taken up the practice of repeatedly relaxing into the present moment, you find it easy to notice the craving as soon as it arises or shortly after.

In noticing a craving, you relax into the natural rest of the present moment, keeping your attention on the inner body. With your body and mind relaxed and awareness alert to the space of the inner body and mind, you notice anytime your mind wanders back into wanting to gamble. This alone may release the energy of craving so it doesn't turn into obsession.

If the cravings start to intensify and you find yourself obsessing, stop for one moment. Think of the SNoRRe method.

Notice the thought about gambling. Noticing interrupts the thought stream. Bring attention into the space of the inner body. Rest and notice the awake and alert awareness within the body.

Let the intense bodily energy that's driving the obsessive thoughts be as it is. Allow it to run its course without trying to manipulate it, modify it, or do anything else with it. Don't put a conceptual label on the energy. Imagine the emotion or other bodily energy filling up the room completely, as if your body no longer has a boundary around it and can no longer contain the energy. Let the energy expand fully into the space within you as well as into the space of the entire room.

If the obsessive thoughts start again—stop, notice, rest, and repeat. Do this again and again in short moments during any obsessive cycle. This releases the Velcro Effect. If you still feel that you may relapse, it can help to call a friend or to go to a meeting where you can get support from others.

A Few Helpful Suggestions

Obsessive energy diminishes naturally by making rest the most important thing in our lives, in all situations, not just when an obsession arises.

Start with less intense energies like slight irritations and cravings. Rest in those moments. This makes it easier to rest when obsession arises.

Key Points

Use the SNoRRe Method Whenever Obsession Arises. When obsession arises, don't try to reason with it. Use the SNoRRe method (it also works well with other extreme states including anxiety and anger). If other methods have worked for you, continue using those methods as well.

Start with Cravings. Cravings are subtler forms of energy that turn into obsession if they aren't noticed when they first arise. Don't treat presence as a remedy you apply only when you find yourself obsessing. Revisit *Chapter Two: Cravings.* Start by noticing the smallest thought and body cravings as soon as they appear throughout the day. Rest in presence when these smaller energies appear, letting them be as they are. The key is to let the bodily energy be as it is, without words or pictures. Starting with smaller craving energies makes it easier to rest during obsession.

Unrealistic Expectation. Don't expect extreme states like obsession and anxiety to magically disappear the first time you use the SNoRRe method. The point of this method isn't to use presence as a quick fix. As the following chapters will explain in more detail, extreme states like obsession and anxiety come from the energy of the self-center. By taking brief moments of rest repeatedly you come to see presence as your real identity. It's this change in consciousness that allows extreme states to naturally relax. This change may be experienced as a gradual relaxation, happening over time.

Remember: Avoid reading this book from beginning to end as if you are trying to learn new information. Notice that there are spaces between each paragraph. Take a moment of rest between each paragraph to really soak in the words and allow them to point you to presence within your own experience. If you begin feeling frustrated with the repetition of certain instructions such as "rest" and "allow all energies to be as they are", it may be that you are using your mind too much. Let that frustration be a reminder to relax and read this book more slowly, treating it as a reminder to experience presence rather than a way to merely feed your intellect with more information.

CHAPTER FOUR
Self-Centeredness

In this chapter, we're taking a closer look at what drives the cycle of addictive seeking and why the natural rest of presence is the key to end this cycle completely, in all its forms.

An Identity Crisis

As addicts, we don't know who we are. We live in an ongoing identity crisis and we're barely aware of it.

During the course of a lifetime, our identities change often. We go from child, to friend, to spouse or partner, to employee, to addict, to recovering addict, to sick person, to dying person. None of these labels are our real identity.

They're nothing more than temporary concepts.

Seeking is based on a desire to find a solid and permanent sense of one's self in time.

We keep looking to the future in hopes that we'll find out who or what we are. We keep looking for that next label, relationship, fix, or awakening.

Yet, we never find the answer. The most we ever find is another label with which to identify.

Natural rest is about solving this identity crisis once and for all.

Through the practice of brief moments of rest, a stability and transparency of body and mind is revealed. The energies of thought, emotion, and sensation come to rest more easily or arise less. That's the stability. This does not occur by making stability a future goal. This stability arises in the present moment through following the tools in this book.

Presence is not a concept. It's the direct and immediate experience of life in the present moment without the veil of conceptual labels.

Look to where the word "presence" is pointing. It's not pointing to thought. It's pointing to the thought-free present space in which life actually happens. This is what we are.

Rest deeply into a silent state of not knowing as often as possible.

We've falsely assumed that our identity resides in thought or in the body. Yet, presence is that which sees each thought and is aware of all the sensations that make up the body.

Aren't all thoughts temporary?

Thoughts are words and pictures that temporarily appear and disappear within presence.

How can you be a temporary word or picture?

Words and pictures tell a story of past and future. Past words and pictures contain the sense of "who I am." Future words and pictures contain the sense of "who I am going to become." These thoughts are all temporary. They arise in a series. The fact that they arise one after another in a series doesn't make them truer. They're still only fleeting concepts that come and go.

Every word and picture that appears within our self-centered stories is appearing to a selfless presence that sees the word or picture. This presence is what we really are, not any of the words and pictures.

Through identification with words and pictures that make up a story, we're seeking in time to fulfill a self that's illusory, a self that's being created by the activity of thinking itself.

Identification with words and pictures makes us feel separate from one another and from the universe. So we go looking for wholeness in the future. Yet, all we find are more words and pictures . . . more thinking . . . which just makes us feel more separate. This leads us to look again for wholeness in the future.

We're constantly looking for ourselves.

This is the cycle of seeking. It's our addiction.

It may not be obvious now, but addiction is more than just a compulsion to use or engage in certain substances and activities in order to feel better. It's based in a deeper misconception about who and what we are.

We've been chasing our own thoughts.

By repeatedly relaxing into the natural rest of presence, we end this chase fully and finally. The identity crisis is over!

The Hamster Analogy

Addicts are like hamsters spinning 'round and 'round on wheels inside their cages. We're constantly seeking something more. This constant seeking keeps us imprisoned inside a loop that keeps repeating itself. The loop is made of words and pictures.

We live with a sense of lack or deficiency, a sense that something's missing. The words and pictures keep telling us we're not good enough or aren't there yet. We keep seeking our freedom in the future, but never find it. We only find more words and pictures that tell us the same story, leading us to seek over and over into the future.

We never fully resolve who we are or what we really want through seeking the future. In not finding real freedom through seeking, our stories feel incomplete. This incompletion is the sense of lack or deficiency. This is a self-perpetuating cycle.

Like the hamster on the wheel, we never actually find the completion we seek. We may find moments here and there where we feel complete or satisfied but we never reach that permanent state of freedom, peace, and contentment that provides an end to the seeking itself.

Like the hamster, we just keep running.

We keep escaping the present moment. We keep following the wheel of time as if it's real, not seeing that time is only thought.

The time-bound story of self is only a series of words and pictures. This story is designed to feel incomplete.

In this story, we're looking for anything that fills the sense of lack that is our constant companion.

Lack is our constant companion for only one reason: we continue fueling the belief that our freedom resides in the future, in the next moment, the next fix.

Do you see the vicious cycle of seeking? It's the *very thought* that the future holds our fulfillment that makes the present moment feel as if it's lacking. (You may want to read that again.)

This one critical insight can change everything. Each time a thought or sensation arises that tells us this moment is lacking something, we can make the decision to rest in presence instead of emphasizing the thought or sensation.

In resting in thought-free presence, we come to realize that this moment is already complete as it is. It's only a thought that appears within this thought-free space that makes us believe something else in the future is needed. This thought is a lie! In allowing the thought to come and go without emphasizing it, we see that presence lacks nothing.

The self that we find in words and pictures can't reach fulfillment. It's not supposed to. That's not its real goal. Its only real goal is to keep chasing an illusory future. Same as the hamster on the wheel, all of its energy is spent running, never reaching complete resolution, only continuing to suffer.

We need look no further than our own addictive backgrounds to see this is the case. We have all the evidence we need to make a decision to try another way.

When the thought arises that says some future moment contains our freedom, we simply notice it come and go, and rest in presence. This is the key! We find that the contentment we've been seeking is already here. We've been continuously overlooking the obvious freedom of presence.

This is the most important thing we can do for ourselves as addicts. We stop telling the lie that the future is the key. We make resting in presence the top priority in our lives. This decision frees us from the cycle of seeking.

An Important Question

Ask yourself this question (it's the most important one you can ask in recovery):

What am I seeking?

You may respond that you're seeking to feel better, have fun, or escape boredom, or to find happiness, freedom, love, peace, good health, material success, or something else—even recovery.

But what are you *really* seeking? Look more closely. If you felt better, you'd actually be experiencing *the end of seeking to feel better.* If you found peace, you'd be experiencing *the end of seeking peace.* If you made lots of money, you'd be experiencing *the end of seeking money.* If you found recovery, *you'd actually be experiencing the end of seeking recovery.*

What we're really seeking is *the end of seeking itself.*

We erroneously believe that the end of addictive seeking can be found within the time-bound, thought-based story of self. Let's take a closer look at why the end of seeking cannot be found in that story.

The Self-Center

In this way of recovery, we call the thought-based story of self that lives in time the "self- center." Calling it a self-center helps us understand what it is and what it does. This understanding helps us see why restful presence is the key to the end of addictive seeking.

The self-center is a set of thoughts moving through time, from past, through the present, and into the future. This story of "me," by its very nature, places the self at the center of life.

The story of past includes our name, history, and thoughts about ourselves including our childhood and background, successes and failures. These are all words and mental pictures. When someone asks, "Who are you?" we're likely to answer by referencing thoughts from the past.

But are you a story?

Are you a set of words and pictures appearing within the mind? What does a story of the past have to do with right now? Isn't this moment where life really is?

We normally emphasize either positive or negative thoughts from the past for a sense of self. The thoughts from the past that we emphasize determine how the present moment looks and feels.

If one refers to himself as a victim, for example, he perceives the present moment through the veil of thoughts from his past victim story. This story is a negative conceptual lens and carries negative emotional energy with it.

When a victim looks at the present moment, his eyes reveal a world full of people and circumstances that aren't treating him fairly. His heart is lonely, sad, and angry.

A victim seeks others who will make this story of being a victim seem true. These others buy into his illusion of being a victim. They feed it. They may play the role of perpetrator or they may just enable him to continue telling the story that he's a victim. This solidifies his sense that he really is a victim.

It's a self-perpetuating story. This is all unconscious. A victim doesn't realize he's doing this. He really believes that life is unfair to him. He believes he really is a victim.

The victim story is unreal. It's only a set of thoughts.

A victim is no different than any other story of self. Every story of self unfolds this way, regardless of the content of the story.

Past thoughts and emotions are carried over into the present moment. They repeat themselves in the future.

Even if one refers to herself in a positive way, something like, "spiritual person," she perceives the present moment through that lens. Her eyes reveal a world in which she believes she's special and others aren't as spiritual as she is.

Although this may be a more positive story, with warm and fuzzy feelings to go with it, it's still only a story. Neither the positive nor the negative stories we tell about ourselves are absolutely true. They're just stories. And all stories, whether positive or negative, make us feel separate from each other. That sense of separateness keeps us seeking out wholeness in the future.

These stories cannot provide the deep and permanent freedom, peace, and contentment that relieve us from the cycle of addiction.

By their very nature, stories are unstable.

In the course of a week, for example, we experience a wide range of ups and downs in our stories. One morning we might feel on top of the world. By the afternoon we may feel really angry because of what a loved one said or did.

The next day we may feel fine. But that night we may experience great anxiety over something coming up later in the week, like a doctor's exam or a work presentation.

In these stories, we identify with whatever thoughts and emotions happen to be appearing at the time. The thoughts and emotions feel stuck together. That's the Velcro Effect. And that's how identification with a self-center happens. It's no wonder we've been reaching for addictive substances and activities to make us feel better. In our stories, we're at the mercy of whatever arises. And, whenever we identify with thoughts and emotions, we're at the mercy of the Velcro Effect.

This way of living offers no stability. As addicts, we tend to avoid the negative feelings and chase after the positive feelings. We often reach for our favorite addictive substance or activity to cover up the negative emotions. The stories, therefore, just perpetuate the cycle of seeking the future. We're seeking some later moment that's free of these negative feelings.

Relying on these stories also limits our freedom in the present moment.

We confine ourselves within a thought box. By relying on these concepts for a sense of self, we limit our capacity to live freely in this moment. To live in a box is to live in a contrived, conditioned, and predetermined way.

We often feel a need to rehash past negative situations and fixate on our reactions to those situations. Unconsciously, we're trying to protect ourselves from experiencing pain again, when and if, similar future situations arise.

This need to self-protect keeps us feeling separate from others. We withdraw emotionally. We play it safe, refusing to be vulnerable and open to life. This mechanism of self-protection obscures the non-attached, non-defensive love available in presence.

We act from memories about whom we are rather than from the total freedom of presence. We often try to predict and plan how we're going to act in some future situation, instead of living in the moment and responding from the heart, from an authentic, uncontrived way of being.

When we carry past labels about ourselves into the present moment, these labels color our present view. They limit what we see and do.

These labels limit our creativity. They keep us focused on ourselves. When we're concerned mainly for ourselves, we can't see a present situation the way it really is. We can't see from someone else's perspective. We can't see the big picture. As a result, true creative action that benefits everyone isn't as available to us.

Constantly living from past concepts separates us from each other.

In these stories, we're more concerned with being special and separate from others than with simply being present with others and with what's happening now.

Separation causes us to feel isolated from one another. Isolation is dangerous for us. In isolation, we're cut off from those who can support us in recovery. It's easier, in isolation, to entertain thoughts of relapse and to act out on those thoughts.

We're neither as good as we think we are nor as bad as we think we are. We're neither positive nor negative concepts. All concepts, positive and negative, appear and disappear within presence.

When we emphasize these past stories for a sense of self, we regularly put our mental attention on thoughts that perpetuate the stories. We stay stuck in a conditioned, self-conscious loop. The past just continues repeating itself into the future.

All stories, by their very nature, are incomplete. When you consult the story for a sense of self, doesn't it always tell you that you aren't "there" yet?

What's "there?"

Where is it?

Have you ever really found it? Did you find it the last time you temporarily satisfied an urge by reaching for your favorite addictive substance or activity?

In the story of "me," the seeking never ends. You never get "there!"

Thoughts within this cycle of seeking are restless. In our more intense seeking moments, these thoughts are firing rapidly, one after the other. They're desperately looking within the story for something else—anything that will provide relief from the seeking.

But the story only perpetuates more seeking. More escaping. More running like the hamster on the wheel. The hamster believes he can reach "there" by running more. It's simply not true. He never gets there. The wheel just keeps spinning.

An addict operates on the same erroneous belief.

When we consult past thoughts within the story for a sense of self, automatically, we look to the future for completion of that self.

Looking to the future for completion is the very definition of seeking. Seeking is addiction.

The more we reach for future relief, the more we perpetuate the sense that life is incomplete right now. This fuels the seeking energy behind our addictions.

By identifying with the past and seeking the future, we overlook the simple joy, wonder, mystery, and natural well-being of the present moment.

Life only happens here in this present moment.

This is impossible to see and experience fully as long as we're constantly emphasizing words and pictures about the future.

An addict is like an escape artist, always looking for something else, something more, and a "there" that never arrives.

The story of "me" is the story of the addict.

The addict is the self-center.

In this story, the self is placed at the center of life. It's all about "me," what I personally lack, need, want, and whether life is treating me well.

The self-center is a story of separation. Within this story, the main character is the self. Everyone else is a separate character whose needs and wants are secondary and incidental to the main character.

This sense of being cut off and separate compels us to use and manipulate others for personal gain.

As a result, we find ourselves in competition and conflict with others, especially those that get in the way of what we're personally seeking.

The competition and conflict bring about feelings of deficiency, lack, resentment, and fear. We then try to avoid having to feel these feelings by looking for some release in the future, usually our favorite addictive substance or activity, or maybe a higher level of material success or praise and acknowledgment from others.

This self-center is concerned mainly for itself. As long as we look to thoughts of past and future for a sense of self, the self-centeredness continues operating. The seeking continues . . . The addiction continues . . . The separation, and therefore, the conflict with others, continues . . .

As addicts, it's no wonder we've spent so much time and energy trying to feel better. We're stuck in a story that's incomplete, a story that's perfectly designed to keep repeating itself. This is a painful way to live.

The Problem with Temporary Fixes

We've been operating under the false assumption that a temporary, pleasurable fix can give us the relief we're really seeking. The fix could be anything from a drug to buying new clothes to seeking praise and attention from others to spiritual experiences.

We can certainly satisfy the sense of deficiency within us *temporarily* in this way. But temporary pleasures cannot provide deep, lasting relief from seeking. In fact, they perpetuate more seeking.

Each time we temporarily satisfy an urge to feel better, we falsely believe our contentment comes from the addictive substance or activity itself. The mind associates relief from seeking with the substance or activity.

Then we're off and running on the hamster wheel, seeking more temporary fixes.

Through resting repeatedly in presence, we start to see what's really happening.

Our contentment doesn't come from the substance or the activity.

When we temporarily satisfy an urge by indulging in an addictive substance or activity, *we're experiencing a brief rest from the seeking toward that addictive substance or activity.*

This is an important insight. We must discover this for ourselves.

This *rest from seeking itself* is what we're really seeking.

True contentment is not temporary.

Repeatedly resting in the present moment provides deep, lasting relief from the cycle of seeking.

We've been trying to avoid the pain of our past or recreate pleasurable past moments. We've been seeking the future to feel better.

We've been returning again and again to temporary fixes. We've been returning to drugs, food, work, shopping, gambling, or some other addictive substance and activity.

Temporary fixes will never resolve a lifetime of seeking.

Temporary fixes are tiny pit stops along the endless path of seeking the future.

This chase exhausts us. It often has a detrimental effect on our health and relationships.

Temporary substances and activities are only symptoms of our real addiction. We're really addicted to thought. We're addicted to incessantly thinking about ourselves including where we've been and where we're going. This thinking is based on a present sense of deficiency. But instead of looking at the story of deficiency and seeing it as just words and pictures, we believe it. And deficiency, because it's accompanied by painful or uncomfortable feelings, makes us reach for more temporary fixes.

In seeking these substances and activities as a source of temporary relief from the sense of lack, we overlook simple presence, which is where stable and permanent relief lies.

The Solution

We've identified that the self-center perpetuates an endless cycle of seeking.

How do we find true freedom from this cycle?

Whenever we seek the future in any form, we're looking to complete a sense of self.

This sense of completion is already available to us through presence.

In this way of recovery, the solution is always the same: *Take brief moments of thought-free rest. Do it often, throughout the day.*

We must discover the benefits of presence for ourselves. We cannot rely on what others tell us. We cannot rely on the viewpoints in this book or our viewpoints about presence or recovery. Recovery is too important to just sit and think about it.

We must take up the practice of repeatedly resting in presence. This provides experiential rest in the present moment—the key to freeing us from the cycle of seeking.

Recovery in Natural Rest Isn't a Seeking Game

We don't want to treat recovery as another form of seeking the future.

Presence isn't self-improvement. We're not trying to improve the time-bound story of self. That would be more seeking.

Many recovery programs make us believe we need to seek the future to find transformation. But seeking is seeking, whether it's seeking the high from a drug or seeking a better, more spiritual version of ourselves in the future.

In treating recovery in this way, our drug of choice simply changes from heroin, work, or shopping to recovery, self-improvement, or spiritual awakening. We're just substituting content. The same dynamic of seeking is present in each of those situations.

Although certain practices are proposed in this book, the practices are designed to reveal present rest, not future attainment.

Each moment of rest is an *end in and of itself.*

Presence Naturally Releases Self-Centeredness

For a recovery program to be successful, it must free us from self-centeredness and the cycle of personal seeking.

This is why presence is the key!

In presence, we become aware of this self-centered "me" story carrying past thoughts and feelings into the present moment. The thoughts and feelings may center on deficiency, loneliness, resentment, restlessness, grief, or some other pain, discomfort, or unease.

We become aware of how this residual energy from the past clouds our view of what's happening now.

We become aware of the painful and uncomfortable thoughts and emotions that lead us to seek relief in the future.

We see that the past never resolves itself through seeking the future.

In awake, restful presence, we notice the conceptual story of "me" whenever it arises, in any form.

This sounds like a daunting task. But all we really have to do is take brief moments of thought-free rest throughout the day. A brief moment is only three to five seconds. It's completely doable. This practice makes it easier for us to see the story as something that comes and goes in presence.

These insights can never be learned from a book. We must discover them for ourselves. This can only happen through the practice of resting in presence, regularly.

Through resting in presence, which is the spacious, awake, alert field of awareness within that sees everything arise and fall, our self-centered story and its game of seeking is illuminated.

The story is seen for what it is: a cycle of personal seeking that cannot and will not end through continuing to search into the future. Seeking cannot and will not end through more seeking. This is pure logic!

By noticing this story, and then resting repeatedly into the thought-free present moment, we're waking up out of this dream of self-centeredness.

Resting and noticing thoughts come and go allows the fog of the past to lift. We begin to see this moment without the words and pictures from the past obscuring our view.

And, as the fog of the past continues to lift, any seeking toward the future naturally and automatically begins to fade. We no longer feel incomplete. We no longer look to the next moment.

How to Notice Thoughts

Presence is a spiritual awakening. Don't let the words "presence" or "spiritual awakening" fool you. Nothing fancy here. No special mystical state is needed.

Being spiritually awake just means being aware of what's happening now in terms of words, pictures, feelings and sensations and seeing that there is no self to be found in any of that. These energies come and go temporarily within present rest.

When we don't see the words and pictures arising now, we remain asleep within the self-centered story. We believe we are the story.

We've been asleep within our time-bound stories all our lives. The self-centered story continues only because the words and pictures within the story remain unseen.

Whenever thoughts remain unseen, we believe them. We have no choice. We're at the mercy of whatever they tell us. They often tell us that the present moment isn't good enough, that we need something else, and that we need to seek the future to find it.

In noticing any thought, we finally have a choice! We can choose to rest in presence in that very moment instead of emphasizing the thought for a sense of self.

How do we notice a thought?

It doesn't happen through more thinking. It doesn't happen through effort.

Throughout the day, as often as possible, we simply notice that we are thinking. We let the current thought come to rest by watching it fade away. As it comes to rest, for a few seconds, we relax without thought.

After a moment of rest, self-centered thoughts are likely to resume. We may go a number of minutes or hours throughout the day without reminding ourselves to rest in presence. When this happens, there's no reason to emphasize thoughts about how we haven't been doing the practice enough. Emphasizing such thoughts just feeds the story, "I'm deficient."

When we notice that we haven't taken a moment of rest for a long time, we just catch that thought and take a moment of rest right now, without referencing the past at all. If we fail to notice a thought or if a self-centered story overtakes us, we see that "not noticing" is also just an energy movement within presence. We allow the "not noticing" to be as it is. We don't turn the inability to be present into another self-centered story.

We're not becoming people with stories about being really good or really bad at being present. We're resting in presence without emphasizing even those stories.

We take it easy on ourselves. This is about no longer beating ourselves up. The most loving thing we can do for ourselves is to relax into the natural rest of presence.

By repeatedly resting in presence throughout the day, our bodies and minds become more relaxed internally. We become alert and aware of the inner space within our bodies and minds. When our bodies and minds are relaxed, the entire world seems more relaxed.

We notice a thought the same way one might notice falling stars in the night sky. At any moment, a star could fall. So we keep attention on the sky.

When we take a moment of rest, we also remain alert to the inner space of the mind in the same way we might watch the night sky. Thoughts arise from this inner space and disappear back into it.

The more we take brief moments throughout the day to naturally rest in this way, the easier it becomes to notice thoughts. We start to experience an automatic, effortless return to this restful presence.

As the moments of rest get longer and longer, our ability to notice thought gets easier and more effortless. From the natural rest of presence, where we're completely relaxed internally, we find that thoughts arise all by themselves.

We're finally hearing the voice in our heads. This voice has been telling us that this moment isn't enough, that life isn't enough. We let that voice tell its lies. We simply rest in presence whenever we notice it.

We find that noticing thoughts starts to happen automatically as a result of resting in presence. From this place of relaxation, we notice words and pictures just as we might notice a movie playing on a theater screen.

In restful presence, we notice that a thought is merely a temporary energy. It appears, hangs around for a while, and then disappears. It has no other power.

Every thought is temporary. There's no exception.

Noticing a thought of the past whenever it arises frees us from the belief that our past controls who we are in this moment. As a temporary arising, a thought doesn't have that inherent power. We give thoughts power by emphasizing them, instead of resting in presence.

Noticing a thought of the future whenever it arises frees us from believing we need something else to happen in the future before we can be at peace. This is a lie.

As we rest more and more in presence, the energy of emphasizing thoughts of past and future can finally relax. These thoughts lose their heaviness. We discover that peace is a natural attribute of presence, not something we find through thinking.

We rest whenever we notice we've been overtaken by words and pictures within the story.

We come to see that we're not the labels we've been placing on ourselves. All conceptual labels stop making sense. We aren't criminals, victims, housewives, addicts, recovering addicts, cancer survivors, secretaries, or stockbrokers.

We continue using these labels in a conventional sense. We're not trying to get rid of thought permanently. That would be impossible anyway.

But we come to see that these are ideas. We're not ideas. Ideas don't heal us. Presence is the source of our healing.

To illustrate, let's revisit the pond metaphor from *Chapter One: Natural Rest.*

The pond has no desire to get rid of the ripples on its surface.

Trying to get rid of thought comes from personal will. It's the seeking mind applying force and effort to achieve the future goal of being free of thought. The invitation here is to *rest* in presence.

We're not distancing ourselves from thought.

The pond cannot distance itself from the ripples.

We're not suppressing thought.

The pond does not suppress the ripples. The ripples are inseparable from the pond and therefore allowed completely. Just as the pond never tries to destroy or suppress its ripples, in presence there is no movement to destroy or suppress thoughts. They are temporary fictions that merely give an appearance of self. There's no permanent, fixed self to be found in any of that movement.

Just as all ripples on the surface of the pond are temporary, we see that all thoughts are temporary.

We allow all thoughts to be as they are, without judging or condemning them. We rest in presence. This allows us to no longer identify with thought.

Just like the pond, presence is totally stable. It's always here. This is why we can trust it completely. We can rest in presence no matter what's happening in life.

We relax our bodies and minds into the space of the present moment and know that nothing needs to be added.

Even if it appears as if something needs to be added, like a drug or some other fix, we relax again. We notice that it's only a thought that tells us something needs to be added. We let that thought pass naturally and then we rest again.

If we start to believe something must be subtracted from our present experience, we notice that it's only a temporary thought that tells us this. We rest in presence.

In noticing the thought, it naturally releases itself back into the source from which it came. It disappears back into the stability of presence.

No thought has the power to destroy, capture, limit, or define the present, spacious awareness in which the thought is happening. Each thought comes and then goes, leaving only the stable, silent presence.

The self-centered story of "me" isn't stable. The thoughts within the story constantly change. This lack of stability in the story is part of the reason we constantly seek the future. We're looking for something that will provide stability for us.

Just as each ripple across the still pond is a movement of the pond itself, each thought is a movement of the still, quiet presence.

This still, quiet presence provides true mental stability.

In seeing this, we find no reason to be at war with thoughts. We still utilize thought for practical purposes, but there's no longer identification with it.

We find every reason to relax more deeply into the stability of presence.

We find our true power and confidence in presence. Presence allows us to be in the world in a selfless, uncontrived way, free of fixed ideas about ourselves and free of the personal seeking toward the future.

How to Notice Emotions

Emotions are energy movements within the body that often arise in conjunction with thoughts. The thoughts and feelings seem stuck together.

When emotions remain unseen, they provide the perfect fuel for thoughts. They drive the incessant thinking about the past and future.

Grief, loneliness, resentment, or sadness often arises in conjunction with thoughts of the past. Frustration or anger arises when we resist something that's happening now. Fear arises in conjunction with thoughts about the future.

How do we notice emotions and bring them into the light of present awareness?

Through the practice of repeatedly resting in presence, our attention is placed in the space of the inner body on a more regular basis. Remember, the space of the inner body *is* the space of presence.

By resting in presence on a regular basis, the space of the inner body becomes relaxed, yet aware of itself and alert to what's happening within that space.

We start to see emotions as soon as they arise within this space or shortly after. We don't try to label the emotional energy. We don't call it "anger" or "sadness."

We simply experience the raw energy itself without attaching any words or pictures to it.

We may not always notice an emotion when it first arises. Instead, we may find ourselves replaying thoughts of the past or emphasizing thoughts of the future. And those thoughts often arise along with emotions that seem stuck to the thoughts. When this happens, we observe the current thought until it fades into the space of thought-free presence. As it fades, for a few seconds, we add no additional thoughts. This moment of rest lets us then bring attention into the body, allowing the emotion to be there without any words or pictures attached to it. This allows the emotional energy to arise and fall into presence without hooking back into the story. This automatically undoes the Velcro Effect.

Whenever we feel an emotional charge in the body, we don't try to modify, neutralize, resist, get rid of, or do anything else with the emotion. We bring attention straight into the energy, feeling it from within, and allowing it to be as it is.

We let the emotion be exactly as it is. We let it run its course completely. We let it dissipate on its own, without placing any mental story on it.

We treat every emotion like a welcomed guest in our home. We wouldn't welcome our guests while also strategizing how to get rid of them.

A welcomed guest is accepted completely and allowed to leave whenever he or she feels like leaving. We don't push the guest out the door.

We treat the space of our inner bodies as our home.

Each emotion is allowed to be just as it is in this space. We let it arise and fall, without emphasizing any thoughts that seek to get rid of it. As it begins to dissipate, we don't try to push it away. We allow it to leave on its own time, in its own way. This is complete acceptance. It ends the movement of seeking the future to feel better.

No emotion has the power to destroy, capture, limit, or define the present spacious awareness in which the emotion is happening. Each emotion comes and goes, leaving only the stable, silent presence.

If extreme emotional states such as anger, resentment, or anxiety appear, it may be helpful to use the SNoRRe method on them.

Through the SNoRRe method, we find that even these extreme states are *nothing more* than energy movements in the body that come and go.

These states once felt like monsters that controlled our lives. In restful presence, we finally see these extreme energies for what they really are—movements of presence like everything else.

By allowing all of these energies to be just as they are, we finally find rest from the cycle of seeking. We stop trying to avoid negative energies and chase positive energies.

In restful presence, we find true emotional stability.

Although this section of the book deals primarily with emotions, not all energies in the body are emotions. Some are sensations such as tightness, resistance, tingling, physical pain or pleasure. Just as with emotions, sensations can feel stuck to certain words or pictures that arise. They feel solid and permanent when we give them a name and then begin to weave a personal story around them. For example, a nameless bodily energy arises and we then label it a "sensation," call it "resistance," and add an entire story to it, such as, "I've been in resistance for years and I'll never be free of this." These names and stories make a mountain out of a molehill.

The mental distinction between "emotions" and "sensations" may be helpful to us when we are first beginning to live life without the addictive substances and activities we once used to escape from these energies. But eventually we begin to see that this distinction is no longer necessary. As we become more acquainted with resting in presence, we can begin to drop these mental distinctions of "sensations" and "emotions" as well as the personal stories around them. After all, words cannot feel the energies. They can only describe them. To feel them directly is to rest without words. This is what allows the energies to move, change, or dissolve.

As long as there is a physical contraction or stuck energy somewhere in the body (e.g., throat, chest, stomach or pelvic area), there is likely to be an addiction of some kind happening. These contractions have been with us for many years, often since childhood. They play a key role in the experience of feeling separate and having to protect ourselves from psychological and emotional pain. These parts of our bodies have been unconscious, which just means that we have not been directly aware of them. We've been distracting our attention away from them including reaching for addictive substances and activities that cover them up or medicate them.

As we rest in presence more, the need to protect ourselves in this way begins to diminish. We feel more relaxed, vulnerable and open. As a result, we may start being more aware of these contractions. Being more aware of a contraction is good news. We can then begin to release it by resting our attention right into the middle of the contraction throughout the day, as much as possible, without putting any words or pictures on it. In resting attention directly in the contraction, we are no longer distracting ourselves from this energy.

Some bodily contractions carry hidden words or pictures with them. We often can't see the words or pictures. They are unconscious. The experience of words and pictures feeling stuck to contractions make the contractions feel more solid and unmovable. The Unfindable Inquiry, discussed later in the book, is an excellent way to begin peeling apart these words and pictures so that we can rest more easily with the felt sensation of the contraction by itself, which helps it release. This kind of deep body work with contractions is vital to releasing addiction. But it is not easy to do on your own at first. We suggest working with a trained facilitator at www.naturalrestforaddiction.com. Facilitators are trained to help you see and release the words and pictures so that the energy of the contraction can begin to release more easily.

Selflessness

To transform is to change from self-centeredness to selflessness.

This doesn't happen by chasing some better version of ourselves into the future. That's only the cycle of seeking.

True transformation happens through simple presence. Through presence, the time-bound self-center that has been chasing the future can finally be seen.

Transformation doesn't happen through buying into more ideas either, including concepts of a future better self.

The teachings in this book are only pointers. The invitation is always to experience the presence to which the teachings point.

Presence is experiential. It must be discovered for ourselves.

Emphasizing ideas about presence isn't enough. Thoughts about presence may help in the beginning to remind us to rest, but they're a poor substitute for actually experiencing the natural rest of presence.

We practice resting even when we find ourselves emphasizing lots of thoughts about presence. We allow even those thoughts to come and go within the natural rest. We must discover the benefits of presence for ourselves to truly appreciate it. We cannot rely on what this book says or what others tell us. We cannot rely on our intellectual viewpoints about presence, spiritual awakening, addiction, or recovery.

Transformation happens through recognizing and directly experiencing thought-free, selfless presence as who we really are in the deepest sense, rather than placing our identity in a conceptual story.

In this way of recovery, we find that presence provides a complete freedom from believing limiting self-concepts. Concepts may still arise, but they no longer feel like who we are.

To live in presence is to be free to experience this moment with fresh eyes, to live in an uncontrived and unconditioned way.

When we live in this moment in an unselfconscious way, without referring to self labels and stories, we're free to experience this moment without the past obscuring our view.

We also stop reducing others to labels and stories.

Yet, we're free to allow each of these thoughts to come and go.

The time-bound, self-centered story of "me" starts to seem less important. We stop acting from a role or story. We start responding from an authentic, uncontrived way of being.

Selflessness reveals itself automatically in presence.

Only through discovering and experiencing the natural rest ourselves can we find what we've really been seeking all along: *the end of seeking itself.* We find it has always been here in the present moment, in the one place we've refused (or forgotten) to look.

Key Points

Notice Thoughts and Rest in Presence. Remember to take brief moments of thought-free rest, repeatedly. Whenever you notice a thought arise from within your self-centered story, allow the thought to gently come to rest on its own.

As the thought comes to rest, relax into the thought-free rest of presence. If thoughts arise whenever you're resting in this thought-free presence, don't move to modify or get rid of them. Just rest again! Do this regularly.

Notice Emotions and Let Them Be as They Are. When you notice a self-centered thought, bring your attention into the space of the inner body and notice any emotion arising in conjunction with the thought.

Let the emotion run its course, completely. Don't seek ways to make the emotion disappear. Don't mentally label the emotion.

As you are resting, bring attention directly into the emotion without words or pictures on it. Letting it be felt without words and pictures on it allows it to move, change or dissolve more easily. Notice the space around the emotion also. Sometimes pictures arise as subtle shapes or even colors around or on the emotions. Look directly at any shape or color and watch it, letting it be as it is. Being aware of it allows it to change or dissolve naturally on its own. When it changes or dissolves, bring attention back into the energy, by itself, and allow it to be as it is without that color or shape on it. To treat emotions this way is to no longer avoid or medicate them. Avoiding or medicating emotions keeps addiction alive.

CHAPTER FIVE: Seeking Energy

In this chapter, we're taking a closer look at more specific forms of seeking energy.

Seeking energy is any movement of energy that propels one toward the future in order to escape negative thoughts or feelings or a present sense of lack.

The content of what we're seeking is irrelevant. It could be anything from drugs, attention, fame, material items, money, a vacation, weight loss, sweets, gambling, future happiness, recovery, spiritual awakening, or enlightenment.

The content is thought-based. At the most basic level, we're addicted to thought. And thought is always either words or mental pictures.

In this way of recovery, we're not focusing on the content of the search. Whether the content of our addiction is cocaine or potato chips, the force behind the addiction is the same. We're only interested in recognizing the energy of seeking itself, no matter what form it takes.

We're illuminating whatever's happening when seeking arises, so it becomes easier to rest in the present moment. This rest provides a stable sense of well-being.

Present lack and seeking energy arise together.

It's only a presently arising thought that tells us we need to find something in the future to fill up the sense of lack that's present now.

Present lack and seeking toward the future through thinking arise together, simultaneously. They're two sides of the same coin.

The lack isn't ultimately real or true. It's only a thought. Thoughts of lack arise within presence. Yet, as these thoughts of lack come and go within presence, it remains unchanged, spacious, free, and complete.

By repeatedly relaxing into the natural rest of presence, thoughts of lack are allowed to come and go freely without any need to follow them or do anything with them. The more we rest, the less we believe these thoughts. The belief that we lack something or that we are somehow deficient releases.

Whenever we make resting in presence the most important thing in our lives and stop emphasizing thoughts of lack, freedom reveals itself as naturally present.

The mechanism of addiction is the movement to escape from the present moment. We want to deal with this movement of escaping, directly. We want to shine a light on it and each of its manifestations. By illuminating the various ways we seek to escape the present moment, relaxing into the present moment becomes natural and effortless.

The Escape Routes

Certain forms of seeking are healthy and necessary for humans, especially seeking things like food, water, shelter, clothing and sex. We aren't referring in this chapter to those forms of seeking that pertain to our basic survival needs. Here we are referring to the incessant, unconscious, addictive movement of thinking about the future as a way to cover up, move away from, avoid or medicate the energies we don't like experiencing in our bodies. Our lives are full of these escape routes.

Escape routes are those areas or situations in our lives in which we encounter negative thoughts or feelings or a sense of lack and then try to escape them by seeking the future.

Until we begin to look at all the areas in which we've been trying to escape, we may not understand that using our favorite addictive substance or activity is merely *one* of the ways we try to escape. There are many others.

In the scenarios below, we're not knowingly escaping. It's more like an unconscious movement, based on the false notion that the future is the key to contentment.

By shining a light on some of the ways we're unconsciously escaping, we make this escaping conscious.

Each time we notice these escape routes arising in our lives, we can relax into the present moment.

Through resting in presence, we come to see that it's no longer necessary to emphasize thoughts of needing to escape the present moment and the negative energies appearing within it.

The following are many of the various escape routes we use to avoid the present moment:

Future Contentment

We have been operating unconsciously on the assumption that our contentment lies in the future. What would contentment look like if it were here now? Wouldn't it be experienced as a sense of present freedom and rest?

Wouldn't it feel natural? Isn't contentment just another word for the absence of seeking contentment?

How do we know contentment lies in the future? The fact is, we don't know.

We assume this only because a present thought arises that tells us some future moment holds the key to our contentment. That thought isn't true. It's a lie. We've believed it for so many years but it's only led us to more and more seeking.

Here's what we don't see in the moment that we emphasize a thought: *the thought itself is the very reason this moment seems lacking.* The presence in which the thought appears lacks nothing.

When we emphasize the thought, it pulls us into seeking mode, and then we're trying to escape into the future again.

We can rest in present awareness by just noticing that thought whenever it arises. This natural rest contains an uncaused contentment and joy that isn't dependent on what happens. This present contentment doesn't play the seeking game.

Boredom

Boredom is cunning. We may find ourselves sitting in a moment in which there isn't a lot of activity. Suddenly it may feel as if life is missing something. But life isn't missing anything. Life is complete and whole as it is.

It's only the thought, "Something else needs to happen," that makes it feel like this moment is boring.

Once we see that boredom is only a thought, we can allow the thought, "Something else needs to happen" to float gently by. We can then rest and notice that thought-free presence lacks nothing. Presence is never bored.

Only thoughts tell the story of a person living in time who's bored and who must reach some imagined future moment where boredom will end.

These thoughts come and go within presence. In seeing that "future" is merely a presently arising thought, boredom is seen to be illusory.

Remember: This isn't about ending thought permanently. That would be impossible. Through recognizing presence, thoughts no longer have the capacity to pull us into seeking. They're then free to appear and disappear . . . without controlling our lives.

Complaining and Blaming

Through resting in presence, we begin to see what's happening when thought is complaining about a present situation or placing blame on others and ourselves.

In that moment, there's resistance to what is.

Resistance is seeking energy. The moment we complain or blame, we're seeking the future again, looking for something different to happen.

The invitation here is to notice the complaining or blaming thought as soon as it arises or shortly after; then take a moment of resting in thought-free presence.

If an emotion of anger or frustration arises with the thought, we place our attention into the space of the inner body. We let that space become aware of itself. We let the emotion be just as it is within the space. We don't place a mental label on the emotion.

We notice any resistance to the emotion. We let the resistance be just as it is. We don't even label or analyze the resistance.

In resting in this way, the complaining or blaming energy diminishes. It transforms itself into presence. In presence, everything is allowed and accepted just as it is.

In total acceptance of this moment, we may still take action to change an unhealthy situation. But our actions are coming from presence, rather than resistance.

Problem-Making

Thought tends to make life into a set of problems. In the story, it's one problem after another. Problem-making creates resistance to life. A human life can so easily turn into a story of constant resistance and problem-making.

In these moments of problem-making, it's easy to reach for cookies, a drug, alcohol, or to go gambling or shopping to cover up the negative feelings associated with the problems.

When we rely too heavily on the rational mind in life, we overlook the simple wisdom available in presence. The rational mind becomes a problem-making machine.

Problem-making is perfect fuel for seeking and escaping. When we make problems through thinking, we're in resistance to the natural flow of life available through presence.

We then look for solutions in thought. We look to the same mind that created the problem. This is erroneous, circular thinking. Again, we become like hamsters spinning endlessly on the wheel, never truly resolving the underlying problem of personal seeking. We create problems through thought and then seek solutions through thought. We do this over and over and over.

We never find any kind of permanent freedom this way. Any solutions we find are temporary. Any freedom or rest we experience when we find a solution is only available until the next problem is created.

We don't usually have to wait long for another problem to appear.

Inevitably, another problem arises because problems are thought-based. For most people, thinking is incessant. Thinking is constantly emphasized so problems are constantly being created.

These problems aren't real. They only seem real because we emphasize these thoughts. Situations certainly arise in life, but none of these situations is actually a problem until the mind begins to obsess on the situation.

The mind adds a layer of negativity to the situation. This turns the situation into a problem. The self-center loves to focus on its problems because problems make "me" feel important and separate.

Once we get into the habit of making life situations into problems, and rely heavily on the rational mind for solutions, we become locked into a cycle of incessant, addictive thinking. We remain unaware of the natural rest available to us in the present moment and its inherent wisdom.

Using the pond metaphor, rational thoughts are like ripples across the surface of the pond. They're temporary, unstable, dualistic movements that cannot provide permanent and stable freedom, peace, and wisdom.

A deeper intelligence, a treasure, lies at the core of our being. This intelligence is accessed through resting in presence, not through emphasizing rational thoughts.

The rational mind has its place. We don't want to discard or try to destroy it. That would be impossible anyway. In restful presence, the intellect and rational mind are included, but not emphasized.

The rational mind isn't the key to freedom. In recovery rooms and drug rehab centers across the world, doctors, engineers, lawyers, and other highly rational thinkers are suffering from addiction like so many others. A highly developed intellect doesn't save us from the cycle of seeking. It's often a contributing factor in our addiction to thought.

There is another way. This way doesn't emphasize the rational mind and its problem-making tendency. Instead, we notice the thought that arises to make a situation into a problem. In noticing that thought, we bring attention into the inner body, feeling any emotional resistance to a situation and letting it be as it is. We don't look to thought to find the response to the situation.

We take a moment of rest. In presence, life isn't seen as a problem. Situations arise but they're fully manageable. Presence reveals a wisdom that the problem-making mind cannot access. The appropriate response to a situation arises automatically in this natural rest.

Praise, Attention, and Acknowledgment

There's nothing wrong with being acknowledged for our accomplishments at work or in other areas of life. This makes us feel confident and confidence is healthy.

But when we rest repeatedly in presence and start seeing what's happening within us, we may realize we've been driven by a desire for others to praise or acknowledge us.

We may see we've been craving attention from others or always trying to please other people. A craving is a craving, whether it's for a drug, attention, praise, or fame. It's still seeking, any way you slice it. It all comes from a personal sense of lack.

What are we seeking when we look for praise, attention, or acknowledgment? Aren't we seeking the diminishment of the sense of lack within us? *Again, it's the thought of needing praise, attention, or acknowledgment that creates the sense of lack.* The lack isn't real. It only seems real because we emphasize this thought.

Whenever we notice a thought wanting to engage in some activity to receive praise, attention, or acknowledgment, we take a moment and relax into the natural rest of thought-free awareness. Notice that this awareness lacks nothing.

In just relaxing into presence, the thought of needing praise, attention, or acknowledgment comes to rest. It's freeing to let a thought of lack just pass by without needing to modify or alter it or even suppress it. When it comes to rest, we see that the space in which it comes to rest lacks *nothing*.

Praise, attention, and acknowledgment are temporary energies that appear and disappear within this presence. They have no capacity to increase or decrease the natural rest of thought-free presence. Because of their temporary nature they cannot provide long-term confidence.

Presence is already complete as it is. Praise, attention, and acknowledgement have no capacity to improve upon what's already complete.

In this seeing, the need for praise, attention, or acknowledgement naturally falls away. We find our authentic, selfless confidence in presence.

Replaying the Past

When we're emphasizing thoughts about the past, we're locked in the story of self-centeredness.

The story of the past always feels incomplete. Maybe we were victimized or abused in the past. Maybe we don't believe we've accomplished what we were meant to accomplish in life. Maybe a bad relationship breakup still haunts us.

In rehashing the past, we're carrying these painful or uncomfortable thoughts and emotions with us in the present moment. To suffer means, "to carry over in time."

To carry these thoughts into the present moment means to identify with them. These thoughts and emotions surrounding the past become our identity.

As we find ourselves identified with thoughts of the past, we very often begin looking to thoughts of the future for completion. The hamster gets back on the wheel. Our drug becomes about seeking a better future once again.

Replaying the past is a form of escape. It's like escaping into a thought world instead of being here in the fresh space of the present moment where life is actually happening.

The solution is always the same: When we notice ourselves replaying the past, we take a simple moment of rest in the thought-free space of now. We let all emotions be as they are in this space without labeling them.

This allows us to see that thoughts and feelings about the past are only temporary, self-centered energies coming and going within presence.

Work

Work can be an escape route in several ways. This includes not only the work we do in our place of employment but also housework and projects at home.

We may look at work as an obligation. We may constantly watch the clock, looking forward to breaks, lunches, or weekends. We may resist work while we're doing it. We may think of ourselves as "stuck in a meaningless job."

Through resting in presence, we see that we're constantly trying to escape boredom, restlessness, and whatever other feelings arise at work. We're seeking those times in which we're away from work. Seeking is seeking, any way you slice it. It's always about the future.

In noticing the thought, "I wish lunch were here already," or "I can't wait until I'm off work at the end of the day," we start to see that *the very thought itself* is creating the boredom, restlessness, or other feelings. *That thought* is the reason work feels like a burden.

Work itself isn't the problem. It's our thoughts about work that create the sense of needing to escape. In noticing these thoughts whenever they arise, as well as the emotions that accompany them, we take a moment to rest in presence. In presence, we're able to take care of the task at hand, giving all of our attention to what's happening at work right now, instead of what needs to happen in the future.

Whenever we notice ourselves entertaining viewpoints about all the things that are piling up at work, we take a moment and rest. We notice that, "Things are piling up," is only a presently arising thought. We bring our attention to the space of now.

This makes work much simpler. Stressing out over upcoming projects drains mental and emotional energy.

All we ever have to deal with is whatever's happening right now. Maybe we're having a phone conversation, shuffling papers, or moving equipment. That's it. In presence, we're much more effective because we're present to what's happening rather than emphasizing thoughts about what needs to happen later.

When thoughts about needing some future moment to happen aren't arising, there's no problem. There's only the present moment. Just working!

This doesn't mean we stay at a job that doesn't fit our needs or utilize our skills. We will know when it's time to leave a job or switch careers. We just have to listen to the silence within. This is where all intuition comes from. Intuition is more than a passing feeling or thought. Intuition is known and experienced on a deeper level. It doesn't come from the busy, analytical mind.

Workaholism is another escape route and it comes in several forms.

Maybe we're using employment and career achievements for a sense of identity. We may feel special about who we are, better than other people who don't have important jobs like we do.

Maybe we don't have that "perfect job" yet, but we feel once we do land that job, we'll look better in the eyes of others.

We may be driven by personal ambition, seeing others as obstacles to overcome on our way to the top of the corporate ladder. We may be obsessed with making money.

We may be obsessed with work itself, staying late, taking work home, or thinking about work a lot even when we're not there.

We're fixating on work like a drug addict fixates on his drug of choice. When we obsess on work, we're often avoiding or trying to escape uncomfortable feelings showing up in other areas of our lives.

In each of these scenarios, we're seeking. We're looking to enhance our self-image, our social status, or fill up our bank accounts. We're looking for more, viewing life through the lens of self-centeredness. We're lost in busy work or fixating on some future goal.

Being enthused about our jobs is great! In this way of recovery, we're not trying to curb inspiration and enthusiasm. We're not making work into an enemy. In fact, in the last chapter of this book, we discuss how selfless presence brings out a natural inspiration and enthusiasm within us, one that's not based in self-centered seeking.

This natural inspiration and enthusiasm are available in those jobs that fit our particular interests. When we do what we love for a living, and make the present moment primary at all times, there's no personal seeking in it. Something larger than self-centeredness takes over.

The invitation here is to simply rest in presence in all situations. This includes resting whenever we notice thoughts that tell us we need to seek the future in our jobs. It's only the thought, "I don't have enough money," "I haven't achieved enough yet," or "I need others to think I'm important," that makes it look like the present moment is lacking.

In selfless presence, we aren't concerned with how others view us or with seeking more of anything.

Through constantly seeking in our jobs, we miss the simple joy of being in the present moment. In presence, we find this seeking isn't necessary. The present moment is already complete as it is. This allows us to work from a place of inner acceptance and simple joy.

Fearful Future Scenarios

We may find ourselves entertaining fearful scenarios about the future.

Perhaps we're afraid of losing a job, experiencing a breakup, divorce, illness, or even death. Perhaps someone or something is threatening our reputation and, therefore, our self-image.

Thoughts may start to race as we desperately project into the future, trying to control outcomes. These racing thoughts are often accompanied with the energy of fear or anxiety in the body, usually in the chest or stomach.

For most of our lives, we've believed that when such fear or anxiety arises, the answer is in the mind. When we project into the future, we're emphasizing thought. In emphasizing thought, we're distracting ourselves from having to actually feel the fear in the body. We're trying to avoid or get rid of the fear or anxiety.

Like all forms of escape, this is an attempt to feel better. It's really no different than chasing after a drug to medicate ourselves.

The invitation here is to fully face this fear or anxiety and stop escaping by projecting into the future. We do this by noticing that the future is merely thought arising in the space of the present moment. The fearful future scenarios we're trying to avoid are nothing more than presently arising thoughts that come and go when we no longer follow them.

By noticing thoughts of the future as soon as they arise, or shortly after, we rest in presence.

As we rest in thought-free awareness, we allow the emotional energy of fear or anxiety to be as it is in the body. We don't label it. We don't even call it "fear" or "anxiety." To label it would be to go back into thought.

Presence is too simple for the mind. The mind believes it's in control. Thought complicates everything. Our own addictive backgrounds are the perfect evidence that the mind isn't the answer to the problem of seeking. It's also not the answer to our fear and anxiety about the future.

Mind only gives us more seeking, more analyzing, more labeling—none of which provide the deep rest that ends seeking and allows fear to relax.

Relying on thought has been our escape route.

The only instruction from the mind we need to follow is "rest in presence." This one instruction changes everything.

Through resting, we're no longer escaping our fear. We're facing it.

In letting the energy of fear and anxiety be just as it is without labeling it, the energy converts itself into presence.

We come to see that fears and anxieties aren't monsters. They're energy movements, like everything else. In facing them, the energy can finally relax.

If the energy returns again, it's seen for what it really is—a temporary, fleeting movement within stable, changeless presence. We allow the energy to come and go without trying to modify or escape it. We simply rest, again and again. In restful presence, fear and anxiety no longer run our lives.

Transferring Emotional Energy

We often avoid facing uncomfortable or painful emotions when they arise and then we try to transfer the residual energy to other people.

For example, you're arguing over the phone with your spouse. You have a headache and the argument is making you upset. You hang up the phone. You then get to work and find yourself being rude to a co-worker. You notice that, on any other day, you wouldn't have reacted to the co-worker in this manner. The co-worker reacts and the two of you get into a heated argument.

In this situation, the anger that arose while you were on the phone with your spouse remained unseen. You had no attention in the space of the inner body when the anger arose. You were completely "up in your head." The emotional energy was carried over into the situation with your co-worker. Remember, to suffer is "to carry over in time." We carry negative energy over in time by emphasizing thoughts about how angry we are at a person.

It may not be obvious at first that this is a form of seeking. But look closely at what's happening. By snapping at your coworker, you were unconsciously looking for a response. You were looking for an outlet for your pain.

You wanted to transfer your pain to your co-worker. This is totally unconscious. You didn't know you were doing it at the time. Anger feeds on anger, just as fear feeds on fear.

You were seeking to feel better, to transfer or get rid of your pain. The problem is that it doesn't work. You didn't find relief from the anger by transferring emotional energy to your coworker. In fact, the altercation with your co-worker just resulted in more pain.

Whenever we notice ourselves arguing with someone or in a heated exchange, we notice the thoughts that arise when reacting to that person. We bring attention into the space of the inner body. We let the anger be as it is. We don't label it.

By being awake to the anger when it arises, it transforms itself into presence. We're fully facing the emotion rather than avoiding it. We're not carrying it over into the next moment, so we're less likely to attempt to transfer it to someone else.

Impatience

Impatience is another escape route. When we're standing in line at the store or waiting in a similar situation, we may believe people should move at the pace we want them to move. We may get stressed out and frustrated when they don't.

This causes us to suffer emotionally. When we suffer, we seek release from suffering. We seek to escape into a future moment when we'll feel better. We aren't facing the impatience directly.

In these moments, we're resisting life as it is in the present moment. We're looking for something to be different, looking for a future moment in which our impatience will fall away.

When people and circumstances do change, our impatience may fall away briefly. We then erroneously believe the relief from our impatience lies outside ourselves in people and circumstances. We become prisoners to what other people and circumstances are doing.

The key to the end of impatience lies in presence. When a thought arises that something should happen at a quicker pace, we simply notice it and direct attention into the inner body.

We notice any energy of resistance there and we let that energy be as it is. We rest in presence. This effortlessly converts the impatience into presence. Our contentment is no longer at the mercy of other people and circumstances. It's ever-present.

Control

Control is a movement to change or manipulate people, other circumstances, or ourselves.

The thought that life should be different than the way it is now is based on the notion that our peace and well-being is dependent on something happening, on some change. Controlling present situations is a way of trying to bring about peace and contentment later. Do you see the seeking that's built into this?

We're again placing our freedom in the future. The unconscious assumption is that if something could just change, we'd be at peace and at rest. This keeps us continuously chasing the future.

The key is to realize that peace, contentment, and freedom lie in the natural rest of the present moment. This isn't something we realize through thinking. It becomes our actual experience in each moment.

The moment we notice that a thought is trying to control a situation, we relax into restful presence. We keep our attention in the inner body for a moment.

We notice any emotional energy there that's appearing to drive the thought. We don't label the energy. We just let it be as it is.

We see that our peace, contentment, and freedom don't depend on changing the situation. In restful, thought-free presence, the need to control naturally releases itself.

Key Points

Spot the Seeking Energy. Seeking energy comes in many forms. Through resting in presence, you become aware of these forms. This allows you to spot them whenever they arise.

Notice Seeking Thoughts and Let Energies Be as They Are. When seeking energy appears, in any form, notice the thought and take a moment of rest. Bring attention into the space of the inner body, letting all seeking and other emotional energies be as they are without labeling them.

CHAPTER SIX: Relationships

Relationships can be incredibly challenging for addicts. In our addiction and self-centered behavior, we may have left behind a string of damaged relationships with people who no longer trust us.

We may have used people for personal gain. We may have even stolen from loved ones or physically or mentally abused others.

We may have placed ourselves in situations where we were victimized or abused by others.

We may find, even in recovery, a desire to isolate ourselves from others. When we're disconnected from others, loneliness and self-pity can take over. We may find ourselves in conflict with others. When conflict is prominent in our lives, we carry around anger and resentment.

When these negative feelings dominate our relationships, we may find ourselves wanting to resort to addictive substances or activities to cover up the feelings. This is why relationships are an important topic in this book.

The ultimate point of this chapter is to help us see through separation itself. When we believe in the notion that we're separate beings, somehow cut off from one another and from life itself, we feel incomplete. We then go looking for wholeness in other people, places, experiences, and things. When this separation is seen through, that tendency relaxes.

We find perfect contentment in presence.

Rest in Relationships

Whatever the case may be with regard to relationship issues, the solution is always the same: relax repeatedly into the natural rest of presence.

Yes, it's that simple!

Presence is selfless by nature. Selfless, compassionate, loving, peaceful, and wise action happens naturally through presence.

In our relationships, we're often operating from self-centeredness. Old patterns repeat themselves in each relationship.

We try to protect, defend, and bolster a self-image. We erroneously believe our thoughts about others are absolutely true. We want to be right and make others wrong.

We desire that our wants and needs be met first, above others.

We may find ourselves locked in a pattern of using, controlling, and manipulating other people or being used, controlled, and manipulated by others.

Each time we respond in a relationship from this self-centered story, we solidify a sense of division in the relationship. It's me vs. you, instead of "we."

This keeps us trapped in the old patterns and locked in self-centeredness.

Self-centeredness leads us into seeking the future for release from the emotional pain that accompanies these relationship issues.

By simply relaxing into restful presence, we see that the self-center we're trying to protect, defend, and bolster in relationship is merely a set of passing mental images. It's merely thought.

Our thoughts about others have nothing to do with them. They're thoughts viewed from within a self-centered story. Others are seen as incidental and secondary to the main character in this story—"me."

Resting and relying on presence in relationships changes everything.

Restful presence is selflessness. We don't need to act as a "selfless person" would act. That's a contrived way of being in the world. It's a story. Selfless presence is much simpler than that. By simply resting in presence in all situations, we automatically and naturally respond in a selfless, uncontrived manner.

Presence is already complete. It seeks nothing from others because it lacks nothing. This is perfect acceptance of self and others.

Selfless presence wants nothing in return for its actions!

We don't need complicated manuals or theories about how relationships work or about how to act toward one another.

We simply, but completely, trust presence in every situation within every relationship.

Through resting in relationships, our self-centeredness is transformed into a desire to be of selfless, loving, compassionate service. No relationship manual can teach us how to be selfless, loving, and compassionate. We already are. We've been overlooking these natural attributes by emphasizing the story of who we are. This story places the self at the center of life.

In relaxing as presence, these attributes shine through naturally and effortlessly. These elements are seen not as something we do or achieve, but as expressions of our natural state of being.

Resistance and Conflict

We may find ourselves in resistance or in conflict with others.

Resistance is energy that arises in the present moment in the form of thought, emotion, or some sensation within the body.

It may be a thought that says something or someone should be different or that someone should stop doing what they're doing or saying what they're saying.

Resistance sometimes arises as the energy of emotion in the body, without any thought accompanying it.

When resistance arises in any form in a relationship, we simply notice it and take a moment to rest in presence.

If resistance arises in thought, we notice those words or pictures and bring attention into the space of the inner body. We let any emotions be as they are in that space without mentally labeling them.

If resistance arises only as energy in the body, without thought, we recognize the space around the resistance. That spacious presence is our real identity. By simply noticing the energy, it can relax. We then allow that energy to dissipate on its own by not emphasizing any thoughts about it. We let it be as it is in that space.

That which notices resistance is presence. Restful presence is already accepting of everything that's happening, both within the body and mind, and in the words and actions of others around us.

In presence, the need to judge others falls away. Resistance and conflict cannot survive in presence.

When we emphasize self-centered thoughts in relationships, we're always trying to protect ourselves from and define ourselves against others. We create an imaginary wall of separation around us. This wall is nothing but thought and emotion. It isn't real.

We come to realize that acceptance doesn't happen when we emphasize thoughts about each other. Thought doesn't accept others. It judges, analyzes, compares, resists, and labels.

Emphasizing thoughts about each other keeps us feeling separate from one another. It keeps us in resistance to each other.

In presence, this separation is seen. The imaginary walls between us begin to disappear. In seeing through these structures, unconditional love and acceptance reveal themselves naturally.

The Need to Be Right

The need to be right in relationships is often a source of conflict.

The need to be right arises from emphasizing thoughts for a sense of self rather than relaxing into restful presence.

The need to be right appears when there's a difference in viewpoints. Regardless of the content of the different viewpoints, the subtext is always the same: "I'm right and you're wrong!" This is an automatic, unconscious response when we take ourselves to be a thought-based self-center.

Being right strengthens the self-center, placing stress on our relationships. When we emphasize the need to be right, we live in isolation and separation from one another.

In these moments, there's an unconscious assumption happening. The assumption is that our identity is contained within thought. By being right, our sense of self is protected, preserved, and strengthened. Being wrong threatens this self-image.

Nothing needs to be analyzed about the need to be right.

Our real identities don't reside in temporary thoughts. So there's nothing to defend with regard to thought. There's nothing to fight about.

Through resting in presence, we find the need to be right diminishes automatically.

No complicated analysis is needed. Only simple rest!

Any emotional energy or sense of diminishment from being made wrong is allowed to simply be in the space of the inner body. This energy transforms itself into presence.

In presence, no defense is needed. Life feels undivided and peaceful. We're not at war with others.

We have no access to who a person is beyond our thoughts about the person. And our thoughts about the person are not the person. They are subjective thoughts.

In restful presence, all thoughts are allowed to be as they are. To allow a thought about a person to be as it is without trying to modify it is the same as allowing the person to be as she is. This is true acceptance.

Presence transforms relationships. It allows all mental and emotional energy to be as it is. It allows others with whom we make contact to relax their need to be right.

Relationships become infused with rest. A natural ease of being permeates each encounter with each person.

We may still take action to help others or change or leave unhealthy situations. We may still explain to others that their behavior is unacceptable. But our response is coming from the natural, selfless wisdom of presence, not from self-centeredness.

Taking the Perspectives of Others

We may find a deep peace through presence. We may see through a lot of our own concepts and stories. We may no longer find the need to incessantly emphasize these concepts and stories.

In this seeing, we want to be mindful of the temptation to tune other people out. Presence isn't about ignoring others' stories. When we tune other people out as they're speaking, we're using thought-free presence as a way to cut ourselves off from life and from others. This is just more escape.

Presence carries a natural capacity to listen without judgment and condemnation of what others are saying.

Presence is already awake and alert, listening to what's appearing.

All we have to do is notice this alertness.

All sounds, words, ideas, and stories appear and disappear within a deep silence.

In all conversations, we listen from silence. Silence is openness.

Simply resting as silent presence allows us to listen fully to what others are saying. This reveals a natural compassion within us.

Within presence, we find a natural capacity to take another's perspective completely and nonjudgmentally.

As someone begins speaking, we allow her words to create concepts within the mind. We notice the thought-free presence of our basic identity is like a blank screen on which her words paint a picture.

As we're listening, we become her story. We put ourselves in her position, as the main character in her story. This is "perspective taking." We're taking the perspective of the speaker.

We don't listen to her story to simply agree or disagree or to give advice, although that can happen.

To be open when someone is speaking doesn't mean that we never disagree with what she's saying. Disagreement happens. But in noticing that we're disagreeing, we become aware of the viewpoint we're emphasizing.

By letting that viewpoint come and go, without emphasizing it, we can relax again into nonjudgmental, quiet restful presence.

This clear, quiet mind is the true listener within us. From this place, we're able to take the perspective of the person speaking.

In listening from nonjudgmental presence, we're able to notice whenever we're agreeing with others just to please them. People-pleasing is self-centered. We're more interested in people liking us than in really hearing what they're saying.

In perspective taking, we listen for listening's sake. We listen for the sake of inhabiting the speaker's story from her point of view. We listen from nonjudgmental silence. Our main interest isn't agreement, disagreement, or even neutrality. Our interest is taking the perspective of the one who's speaking. For that moment, we become the speaker.

In perspective taking, we allow the speaker's words to become a movie within our minds, regardless of whether the story is pleasant or unpleasant, or whether it feels right or wrong. We allow each scene to play out completely. She's the director and producer. We're merely the screen for her script.

If she begins telling us about her day, we allow those words to create the story of her day as it's playing out. We feel into her emotions as best we can.

If she's explaining the frustration she experienced while arguing with her husband, we place ourselves there, in her shoes, during the argument. We look from her eyes as she tells the story. We see her husband from her point of view. In that moment, we see everything from her point of view.

If she's telling the story of how wonderful it was to walk in the park on a cool autumn morning, we place ourselves there, in her shoes, walking through the park, seeing the beauty of nature through her eyes.

Every person we meet becomes a new perspective for us to take. We come to see that life contains many perspectives.

Perspective taking is a deeply compassionate form of sharing. It's true sympathetic listening, unencumbered by judgment and criticism. It opens us up to seeing life from many angles. It opens us up to the unconditional love already present within us.

The possibilities are limitless in perspective taking. A partner can take the perspective of his significant other. A defendant in a criminal case can take the perspective of the judge. A mother can take the perspective of her addicted son. A Christian can take the perspective of a Muslim.

A twenty-year-old can take the perspective of a sixty-year-old. Someone completely healthy can take the perspective of someone dying of cancer. A male can take the perspective of a female. A heterosexual can take the perspective of someone who's gay or lesbian. A heroin addict can take the perspective of a housewife addicted to shopping.

When we open up in this way, we stop looking at life from within a self-centered lens. We start looking from what we really are—selfless love. We see that presence takes a vast array of forms and that only our stories separate us. In selfless love, the boundaries between us are seen to be conceptual only and so they dissolve.

When we don't take the perspectives of others, and we only look from our own perspective, we live in a self-centered reality. We consult only our own thoughts. We dismiss those that disagree with us or present a different interpretation. When we meet people, we're meeting interpretations of life that are very different from ours. In self-centeredness, each person lives in his or her own reality.

It's only the emphasis on thought that separates us, making us feel as though we live in separate realities.

As we're taking the perspective of another, we may find that a certain response is necessary or that there's something we feel we need to say in order to help the person speaking.

We may still find it necessary to agree or disagree or give advice. This is perfectly fine. We retain the ability to use our discriminating minds when necessary.

When we do respond, we respond in presence. By relaxing into presence before, during, and after our response, the response comes from selflessness. It's naturally infused with rest, wisdom, love, and compassion. It isn't coming from the seeking, controlling, and manipulating energy of the self-center. It isn't coming from a need to be right. It's coming from openness.

We know that when we're speaking, we aren't being objective. We're merely stating a single, limited, subjective point of view, conditioned by our particular language, personal history, values, and cultural, religious, and philosophical framework.

In selfless presence, we're fine whether or not other people listen to us or take our suggestions and advice. We lose the need to be heard and be right. We find a natural desire to hear and remain open. These attributes don't need to be cultivated through effort. They arise naturally through making restful presence the most important thing in our lives.

In the openness of presence, there's nothing we need to change about others or ourselves. We simply rest in selfless presence, listening without judgment and responding naturally from that presence.

The transformation of our relationships happens effortlessly through presence.

Uncontrived openness is quite natural. All we have to do is notice this openness. As we rest in presence, it simply makes itself available.

True wisdom and the right response in any situation arise naturally when we look first from the perspective of the other person. When we relate chiefly through agreement and disagreement, without attempting to look from the perspective of the other person, we're reacting from only our own perspective. In this reaction, there's often a false assumption that we see a situation the way it really is. But without taking another person's perspective, we are—by definition—*not* looking outside our own perspective. We're merely repeating ideas we've learned. We're not engaged in compassionate, active, wise listening. As a result, our creativity and ability to look freshly at a situation are stifled.

In those moments when we're reacting solely from our own ideas, without taking the perspective of others, we often fail to understand what's being communicated fully including all the facts, viewed from many angles of those involved. In order to act in the best interests of others, we have to see a situation, as best we can, from other people's perspectives, not only our own.

In perspective taking, we move beyond the separation and conflict inherent in the "I'm right/you're wrong" knee-jerk mentality of the self-center. Selfless action naturally appears. Love and compassion flourish.

Shadows

Have you ever seen a trait, emotion, or other attribute in someone else that really bothered you?

Have you ever seen a trait, emotion, or other attribute in someone else that you found yourself extremely attracted to, perhaps even to the point of obsession?

These are shadows. Shadows are aspects of the self-center that get repressed and then projected outward onto others. These aspects are either too ugly or too beautiful for us to own.

Shadow boxing is the act of being persistently bothered by and reacting to some negative trait you find in another person. It can be a character trait or an emotion.

For example, imagine a neighbor is really nosy. She seems to want to be in everyone's business all the time. If her trait of nosiness really gets under your skin, it's likely a shadow of your self-center.

In this scenario, the trait of nosiness is a negative trait you don't believe you possess or don't want to possess. And so you repress it. Once it's repressed, it starts to appear in others. Suddenly, it's apparent that someone is really nosy but it's not you! It's your neighbor.

Why does this particular trait of nosiness in your neighbor bother you? Why don't other traits in people bother you this much? Nosiness really gets under your skin because you believe you're not nosy. You've been telling that story. Yet nosiness remains a repressed aspect of your own personality. So it's projected onto others. When you pick at your neighbor for being nosy, you're boxing your own shadow.

Shadow hugging is the opposite. It's the act of being persistently attracted to or even obsessed with a positive trait you find in another. It can be a character trait or an emotion.

For example, imagine your boss has an amazing ability to speak with total confidence to a group of people. You're highly attracted to this trait in her. In comparison, perhaps you see yourself as someone who's shy or nervous around others. It's likely that this trait of confidence in your boss is a shadow of your self-center.

Shadows often appear in this way, as opposites. We own one side of the opposite and project the disowned side onto other people.

In this scenario with your boss, the trait of confidence is a positive trait that you possess, but you've repressed or disowned it. You believe you don't possess the trait. So it appears predominantly in others. You find yourself attracted to this trait of confidence more than other positive traits you see in others. In idealizing your boss, you're hugging your own repressed shadow.

Shadow boxing and shadow hugging result in disharmony within us and in our relationships.

The 3-2-1 Shadow Process

Re-owning shadows allows one to rest more deeply in presence. Shadow work isn't a prerequisite to resting in presence. We don't have to search out all the shadows in our lives before starting the practice of resting in presence (see "Turning Natural Rest into Busy Work" in *Chapter Nine: Misconceptions and Traps*).

Prior conditions or causes aren't necessary precursors to relaxing into the natural rest of the present moment. Remember, restful presence is available always, in the here and now. It's unconditional and uncaused.

But if continuous conflict and stress exist in our relationships due to unseen shadows, then we can benefit from shadow work. Shadow work can help relax the sense of division in our relationships. When we're mentally fixated, in one way or another, on good or bad traits in others, it may be difficult for us to take moments of resting in presence. We're just too busy emphasizing stories about who we think other people are.

Shadows are deeply embedded aspects of our own personal stories. These aspects are repressed and projected outward onto others. To re-own or reclaim a shadow means to relax the conceptual boundary between self and other. In shadow work, this boundary is sometimes called the "repression boundary."

The repression boundary is one of the bases for the division in our relationships. This division causes conflict and stress. Conflict and stress bring about negative feelings. As addicts, we have a tendency to want to cover up or escape negative feelings by reaching for our favorite addictive substance or activity. That's why shadow work is helpful in recovery.

Simply noticing a shadow when it appears isn't enough to see through the repression boundary. We can notice shadows appear and disappear all day long and they'll just keep appearing and disappearing—torturing us. Shadows, by their very nature, are repressed and unseen. They always appear as an "other." Therefore, noticing thought isn't likely to reveal a shadow.

Even resting in presence isn't likely to reveal shadows. In resting in presence, we absolutely become more able to see our self-centered story. But the problem is that shadows don't appear within our stories. They're repressed aspects of our stories, projected onto others.

Without shadow work, we just keep boxing and hugging these shadows.

This book employs the 3–2–1 Shadow Process developed by the Integral Institute. The Integral Institute is an organization founded by philosopher Ken Wilber. It's devoted to assisting in the evolution of human consciousness and helping humans integrate various perspectives. The 3–2–1 Shadow Process includes three parts:

(1) *Spotting the shadow,*
(2) *Dialoguing with the shadow, and*
(3) *Re-owning or reclaiming the shadow.*

Spotting the Shadow

Spotting a shadow is easy. Once you notice there's some trait, emotion, or other attribute in another person that really bothers you or that you're highly attracted to, you've spotted a shadow.

Dialoguing with the Shadow

To dialogue with the shadow means to speak to the disowned trait and to discover the reasons why you find yourself either repelled by or attracted to the trait. You can do this mentally or write it out. Shadow work can also be done with a partner.

If you're doing shadow work alone, you act out both voices in the dialogue; that is, you play the part of the questioner and the trait itself.

If you're doing shadow work with a partner, your partner acts out the role of the disowned trait.

Let's return to the nosy neighbor scenario. Dialoguing would happen this way:

You: Why are you so nosy?

Trait of nosiness: Why? Because nosiness is what I am and what I do. I have no other reason for being in this universe other than to be nosy. Being nosy is my business because I'm the trait of nosiness.

You: But don't you see you're invading my privacy and it's disrespectful?

Trait of nosiness: Of course it's disrespectful. Have you ever heard of respectful nosiness? My entire reason for being in this universe is to disrespect your privacy and to be involved in your business. After all, I'm the trait of nosiness!

Re-owning the Shadow

Once you've dialogued with the shadow, it can be re-owned or reclaimed.

What does it mean to re-own the shadow? Specifically, it means to look at your own story, what's happening within your thoughts, and to see that the very trait you're reacting to in the other person is a trait that operates within your own story.

It means to actually *re-own* the trait, to reclaim it. Say to yourself, "I am nosy!" and MEAN it! Actually list the ways in which you've exhibited the very trait you're boxing (negative) or hugging (positive) in other people.

Own this aspect of your story you've been repressing. Feel how that feels, to own what you've been denying. By re-owning it, the self-deception ends. The trait stops being repressed and projected outward onto someone else.

In re-owning the trait, it becomes easier to rest in presence. Of course, the point isn't to start telling the story that you're nosy.

The point in re-owning the shadow is to see both stories: the "I am not nosy" and "I am nosy" stories are both equally coming and going in presence. And, in presence, neither story is emphasized.

The disharmony in relationships relaxes as you see that you're ultimately neither the trait of nosiness nor its opposite. You're the space of restful presence in which both these energies (and all other energies) appear and disappear.

Shadows can also appear as emotions.

For example, let's say you've taken up the practice of resting in presence throughout the day. Through resting, much of your anger has dissolved. You just don't find yourself getting angry with your partner much or flying off the handle when a fellow driver cuts you off on the freeway.

Very subtly, you begin to believe you've transcended or worked through all of your anger. You begin telling yourself you're not an angry person.

But suddenly, everyone else seems angry. Your wife seems angry. Your boss always looks mad when he's telling you what you've done wrong at work. This really bothers you. You ask yourself, "Why is everyone so angry? I'm not angry, but everyone else is."

Imagine one day you're having a discussion with your boss and his anger starts to really get under your skin. His face gets redder and redder. You tell yourself you're perfectly calm but your boss really has an anger problem.

Maybe your boss is angry, but why does it bother you so much?

Chances are you're shadow boxing. You aren't aware of the anger inside your body during the discussion with your boss. In re-owning the emotion of anger, you stop shadow boxing that emotion in everyone else. Suddenly, it no longer looks like everyone else has an anger problem.

This is why we suggest in this book to let all energies be just as they are. We don't try to get rid of anything. We don't suppress anything. In letting emotions and traits be as they are within us, we don't repress, suppress, disown, or get rid of them. So there's less chance that we'll shadow box these emotions and traits whenever they appear in others.

External / Internal Shadows

We often don't see that, when others confront us and we get defensive, the others are simply presenting an unseen, repressed aspect of our personal story.

External pressure from others is internal pressure. We call that the *Pressure Shadow.*

External criticism from others is really internal self-criticism. We call that the *Criticism Shadow.*

Let's go into more detail about the Pressure Shadow and the Criticism Shadow.

The Pressure Shadow

It may not seem obvious at first, but *all external pressure is internal desire.* Let's illustrate this with an example:

For the last several years, John has been meaning to paint his house. In the last year, painting the house fell off John's priority list. Other things became more important, like work and his hobbies. His drive to paint the house never actually left. It just became overlooked, repressed. It stopped appearing as a conscious story or desire within him. One day, John's wife says, "I thought you were going to paint the house! It looks awful! Are you ever going to do that?" John gets very defensive, "Stop nagging me!"

John doesn't see that this is a shadow. To John, it's his wife's problem. She's nagging again. John thinks, "If she would only stop nagging, everything would be OK!"

John doesn't realize that his defensiveness carries great wisdom. The external pressure he feels from his wife is really an internal, unmet desire. It's revealing or drawing back into awareness his own internal, unrealized desire to paint the house. His plan to paint the house was forgotten. It became repressed. That's all.

John's wife is just reminding him of his own desire to paint the house. But because John doesn't see it for what it is—forgotten or repressed internal desire—he mistakenly feels it only as external pressure. It's experienced as an "other." So instead of "I have a desire to paint the house that I forgot about," it's interpreted as "my wife is pressuring me again."

A lot of relationship conflict can be attributed to not seeing the Pressure Shadow. The 3–2–1 process works well with the Pressure Shadow. Re-owning the Pressure Shadow can help us see how the other person we're in conflict with is really our own disowned shadow voice.

In the example above, restful presence is more available for John once the Pressure Shadow is re-owned; consequently, the conflict John feels toward his wife drops away. How does John re-own the shadow? He says to himself, "I have a desire to paint the house!" He feels *into* that repressed desire completely. He remembers that it's *his* desire. Then he rests in presence.

The Criticism Shadow

All external criticism is internal self-criticism. For example, let's say someone calls you "greedy" and you get defensive. It could be any trait: materialistic, self-centered, arrogant, or unintelligent. This appears as external criticism because it's coming from someone else.

The position of defensiveness always offers us great nuggets of wisdom. Your defensiveness is revealing that you're carrying around a self-critical story. You have a repressed story that *you're greedy.* You see greed as an ugly trait, one you can't imagine exists within you.

With the criticism shadow, you're criticizing yourself through the other person.

You get defensive precisely because you've felt and experienced greed before, but have disowned it as a character trait. If there was no identification with the thought, "I am greedy," then someone calling you greedy wouldn't provoke a defensive reaction in you.

Next time someone criticizes you and you experience a defensive reaction, thank him or her for revealing that you've repressed the story, "I am greedy." Instead, you've been telling an opposite story, which is "I'm not greedy."

Spot the shadow. Dialogue with it to see exactly how it makes you feel when you hear the external criticism. Then see it for what it really is—internal self-criticism. Re-own it. Say to yourself, "I am greedy" and MEAN it. Then rest in presence, allowing any emotional energy that accompanies that thought to be as it is.

In re-owning the criticism shadow, there's no one there to get hurt. There's just a seeing of the story, "I am greedy" and whatever feelings come with that story. Both "greedy" and "not greedy" are seen to be equal energies in restful presence.

All other dualistic energies are equally allowed to be. We're no longer at war with any of these stories, traits, emotions, or other energies. We're no longer owning only certain energies and disowning others.

This allows us to rest, deeply and profoundly, as presence.

Presence transforms every relationship. To love is to live without divisions. To box and hug shadows is to live in a divided way. When we shadow hug, we're idealizing others, seeking to be like them, and avoiding our own natural goodness. When we shadow box, we remain in conflict with others, criticizing the very trait we cannot see within ourselves.

Through shadow work, we see that these thought-based divisions finally come to rest. We stop emphasizing and fixating on the positive and negative traits of others. We rest fully in presence, letting these thoughts be seen for what they are—temporary energies that never form a solid, separate self or other.

Think of shadow work as an extra tool in your toolbox. It complements the practice of resting in presence. Why is shadow work helpful? When we find ourselves shadow boxing or hugging, we may experience emotional upset. That emotional imbalance is often what leads us to pick up an addictive drug or activity to cover up or medicate those emotions.

CHAPTER SEVEN: The Living Inquiries

The Living Inquiries are the *most potent* tools in this book. Many people have discovered freedom using these tools. They free us from our addiction to self and from the disharmony and imbalance we experience in certain relationships with other people. They work very well to clear away the stories that lead us into addiction and keep us addicted. The Living Inquiries are best done with a trained facilitator first. These facilitators are trained to help you avoid certain traps you may experience when trying the inquiries alone including not sitting with energies in the body fully or using your mind too much in the inquiry, which unnecessarily complicates the inquiries. Once you have done the inquiries with a facilitator a few times, it is easier and more effective to try them on your own. For more information about the inquiries and to find a facilitator, visit www.livinginquiries.com.

The Compulsion Inquiry

A very effective tool for stopping the compulsive use of substances and activities is the Compulsion Inquiry (the "CI"). It's recommended that you use this inquiry, as well as the rest of the inquiries in this chapter, with a trained facilitator at first. You can set up private sessions with a facilitator at www.naturalrestforaddiction.com. These inquiries are interactive, which means that their true effectiveness comes to life only when a facilitator is guiding you directly, gently, and properly through the process.

The CI targets compulsion directly. Before reaching for an addictive substance or activity, an unconscious, ghost-like mental picture (the "ghost image") flashes quickly in and out of awareness. That picture appears as a future thought associated with indulging in the addictive substance or activity. The picture creates a strong, almost instantaneous, body-mind compulsion to use the substance or activity.

The facilitator will teach you how to spot the ghost whenever it arises and how to look at each thought and bodily energy separately in order to release the compulsion. Some people mistakenly think that the CI is about willpower. The facilitator will show you that it is not about willpower. It's about compulsion energy naturally falling away through this process, on its own time. There are many other subtleties in this process that only a facilitator can reveal for you. The facilitator will take you through this process several times in sessions before you begin doing it on your own.

An Example of the Compulsion Inquiry

Tanya: I'd like to use the Compulsion Inquiry on my addiction to donuts.

Facilitator: Ok, what I'm going to do first is induce the craving for donuts in you. Wouldn't you like to eat a donut after this session?

Tanya: Yes, that would be nice!

Facilitator: Did you notice that, when I suggested the donut, a subtle mental picture arose?

Tanya: Yes, I saw the donut.

Facilitator: That picture of the donut is the ghost image. When it appears, it can feel as if there is a *command* somewhere in your experience, compelling you to eat a donut. A command is like a strong urge or desire, creating the sense that you MUST eat it. It's almost as if you have no choice. Pull that particular ghost image back up and sit quietly in presence, staring at the picture very directly. Where's the command to eat a donut in that particular ghost image?

Tanya: I don't know what you mean. I see the picture and I want a donut. Are you saying there is some verbal command somewhere?

Facilitator: Not necessarily a verbal command, like words. Instead, it may be just a sense that somehow the picture *itself* is commanding you to eat a donut.

Tanya: Ah, yes. That's what it feels like.

Facilitator: There really is no command in the picture. It's just a picture. For example, look at the mental picture of a bag of rocks. Does that picture carry a command to eat the bag of rocks?

Tanya: <laughing> No, not at all.

Facilitator: Do you see that, when you look at the picture of the bag of rocks, there is no craving or other energy coming up in your body?

Tanya: Yes, I see that.

Facilitator: Ok, now look back at the picture of the donut. Does that picture seem to carry a command to eat the donut?

Tanya: Now I see what you mean. Yes, it does. Even though I know it's just a picture, like the bag of rocks, something about it seems to be commanding me to scarf down a donut.

Facilitator: That's because there is now energy arising in your body along with the picture of the donut. Do you notice that?

Tanya: Yes!

Facilitator: Now, disregard the mental picture of the donut. Let it fall away and rest in thought-free presence. Bring awareness into your body of the energy that's now arising in there. Before we go to that sensation, first look for *any picture or shape of that area of the body* where the sensation or emotion is. Do you see that picture?

Tanya: Yes, I see a picture of my stomach with a contracted sensation in it.

Facilitator: Stare very gently and directly, without words, at that picture of the stomach. Where is the command to eat a donut *in that picture of your stomach*?

Tanya: There is no command. It's just a picture of a stomach.

Facilitator: Now let that picture of your stomach dissolve. Just relax in thought-free, still, quiet awareness. Feel directly into the *pure energy* in the stomach area, without words and pictures on it. Where is the command to eat a donut in that pure energy?

Tanya: Nowhere. Wow! It doesn't seem connected to donuts. It's releasing now.

Facilitator: But wouldn't you like to eat a donut after this session?

Tanya: It seems like the words you said made me want a donut but the energy in my body is not as strong now.

Facilitator: Ok, imagine the words, "Wouldn't you like to eat a donut," on a large billboard. Sit quietly and look at those words. Where is the command in those words? Which letters of that phrase seem to carry a command? Is it the first ten letters, the letters "e-a-t"? Where is it?

Tanya: Those are just letters, just words. There is no command there.

Facilitator: But you'd like to eat a donut?

Tanya: A little bit.

Facilitator: So you saw a ghost image flash in your mind again of the donut?

Tanya: Now that you say that . . . yes.

Facilitator: Bring that donut picture back up and stare at it in still, quiet awareness. Where is the command to eat a donut in that picture? Look everywhere on the surface of the picture, at every detail of it, without adding any words to what you are seeing.

Tanya: It just looks like a picture. I don't see a command *in* the picture but there is a subtle craving energy in my stomach again.

Facilitator: Bring awareness back to that part of the body where the craving is. Is there a picture of the stomach again?

Tanya: No, just energy.

Facilitator: Where is the command to eat a donut in that energy when you look at it without words?

Tanya: <laughing> Nowhere, and now the craving energy is relaxing.

Facilitator: Would you still like to eat a donut?

Tanya: No . . . wow . . . that's amazing. I just lost the desire for a donut. There is just peace here now. You mean I can do this anytime my donut compulsion comes up? Will I have to do this forever?

Facilitator: You won't have to do it forever. This inquiry has a way of releasing the compulsion for good if you stick with it a while. Don't rely on willpower. Just use the inquiry. Spot the ghost image and then look at it. Ask yourself, "Where's the command in that picture?" Then do the same for any pictures in the body and also for the energy itself without words and pictures being projected onto it.

Tanya: Got it. Thank you so much.

Notes about the Compulsion Inquiry

The Compulsion Inquiry can be done with any substance or activity. You can look for the command in anything that involves *a compulsive movement towards the future* including towards alcohol, a drug, pornography, obsessive cleaning of your house or anything else.

If the word "command" does not resonate with you, you can substitute it with some other word that does resonate, like urge, drive, impulse, need, or desire. You just have to find a word that really captures what compulsion really feels like in your own experience.

If you find yourself overcomplicating the Compulsion Inquiry, just remember this: **three elements, one question.** There are only three elements to look at (words, pictures and bodily energy). Remember, energy is either emotion or sensation. There is only one question to ask (Where's the command?) stated in different ways depending on what you are looking at during the inquiry:

"Where is the command on those words (to drink beer)?"

"Where is the command in that picture (to drink beer)?"

"Where is the command in that energy (to drink beer)?"

The Unfindable Inquiry

The Unfindable Inquiry (UI) is a unique tool that can be used to see through the sense of separation in whatever form it takes. This inquiry goes deeper than many other inquiries in this book. At first, it may be a bit daunting to attempt this inquiry on your own. If you have difficulty, find someone in your Natural Rest group or a facilitator who has experience with this particular inquiry to guide you. Once you get a feel for how it works, you can then begin using it on your own, either by writing it down on paper or practicing it within your own direct experience as you look at words, pictures, and bodily energy. When used properly, the UI is very effective.

The UI can be used in many different ways, as you'll see below. It can be used to see through the sense of a separate self, which means to see the "emptiness" of the self. It can also be used to see the emptiness of another person with whom you're in a relationship or a substance or activity toward which you feel a craving or addiction. The word "emptiness" refers to the fact that, when you actually look for a separate, permanent person or thing, you only find words, pictures and energies appearing, one after another. The object is actually *unfindable* as something separate from these temporary arisings.

The seemingly physical nature of bodies and other objects can be tricky. It can seem, when you first start doing inquiry, that physical bodies and things are more than words, pictures and energy. For example, touching a chest makes it appear that you are touching a solid, separate body or seeing colors and shapes everywhere seems to prove that reality is made of separate things. But having a facilitator guide you through the process helps a lot. Facilitators can show you in your own direct experience that touch and vision are sensations only and that words and mental pictures play a key role in the belief that people and things are separate. Don't try to understand what is being said here intellectually. The UI is an experiential approach. Reach out to a facilitator. You'll be glad you did. This experiential approach is quite freeing because addiction and suffering come directly from the belief in separation and the UI is designed to help you see through that belief.

Here's how the UI works:

1. *Name the object that appears to be separate.*

2. *Try to find the object.* Go through each of the main words, pictures and bodily energies (one by one) that make up the object. For each appearance ask, *"Is this it?"* (Are these words the object? Is this emotion the object? Is this sensation the object?) If you're looking for the separate self, you may substitute the words "Is this it?" with "Is this me?"

Just remember: *"Name it, then find it."*

An Example of the Unfindable Inquiry

Facilitator: Name the object you would like to try and find.

Matt: I'd like to find me, the self-center.

Facilitator: OK, but let's be a little more specific. There are millions of selves in the world, who do you take yourself to be exactly?

Matt: I've always thought of myself as a failure. I'm never going to succeed. I'm miserable most of the time. Yesterday is a good example. I sat around all day just feeling sorry for myself.

Facilitator: So let's say that the object you're trying to find is "Matt," the person who is a failure. Try to find it. Rest in presence and listen to the voice in your head as it says the word "Matt." Is the word "Matt," you—the failure?"

Matt: No, that's just a name, just a word.

Facilitator: How about the words "I'm never going to succeed?" Is that you—the failure?

Matt: Is that me? No, that's just a thought, too.

Facilitator: Be careful not to answer only with the intellect. Look directly with awareness. And remember to pay attention to your body. Does the body react in some way when you see or hear the words "I'm never going to succeed?" If the body reacts in any way, say "yes." If it doesn't, say "no."

Matt: Yes, there is sadness and a contraction in my chest.

Facilitator: Observe the words, "I'm never going to succeed" until they fade away. As they fade away, rest in thought-free presence. Bring attention to the raw energy of sadness and contraction, without labeling it. Take your time.

Matt: OK, I'm sitting with that energy.

Facilitator: Is that energy, by itself, you—the failure?

Matt: No, that energy is not the failure. And it just dissipated once I saw that.

Facilitator: Did you see how the words, "I'm never going to succeed" initially felt stuck to the emotion?

Matt: Yes.

Facilitator: That's the Velcro Effect. You allowed the emotion to be as it is, without the words, and that released the Velcro Effect. Did you notice that?

Matt: Yes. Very nice. Most of my life I've just stayed in the story instead of feeling the emotions directly.

Facilitator: Now I want you to take a moment and rest in presence again. This time, look directly at the words, "I'm a failure." Do you see those words?

Matt: Yes.

Facilitator: Are the words "I'm a failure" you?

Matt: Yes, those words are me. They feel really close . . . too close. The sadness is back.

Facilitator: Let those words relax and feel the raw energy of the emotion without a label for it. Is that energy, by itself, the failure?

Matt: Yes. For some reason, those words really feel stuck to the emotion.

Facilitator: That's OK. Take this pen and paper and write down the words, "I'm a failure." Then look at the words on the paper. Are those words *you?*

Matt: Now I can see that they're just words. No, those words are not the actual failure. The emotion released as soon as I saw that.

Facilitator: Put the words "I'm miserable most of the time" in a picture frame in your mind. Are those words you—the self that's a failure?

Matt: Yes, that definitely feels like me. The sadness and contraction are back.

Facilitator: Look at the words, "Sadness and contraction." Are those words, by themselves, the failure?

Matt: No, those words are not it, not me. But the words, "I'm miserable most of the time" seem like they are me, the failure.

Facilitator: Whenever any thought *feels* like the object you're trying to find in this inquiry, it always means that some emotion or sensation is arising along with the thought. Emotions and sensations are like alarm bells reminding you to be in your body, and to feel the emotions directly. So relax all words and pictures and just rest in presence. Bring attention directly to the nameless energy in your chest. Take as much time as you need. Relax and let that energy be as it is. Is that energy you, the failure?

Matt: That energy feels like me.

Facilitator: OK, whenever an emotion or sensation feels like the self, it just means that some thought (i.e., some words or a mental picture) is arising along with it. That's the Velcro Effect. What words or picture appear?

Matt: It's a memory of me losing my last job.

Facilitator: OK, that's a picture. Look directly at the picture of you losing your job. Is that picture, by itself, you, the failure?

Matt: No, that's not the failure. The picture just faded.

Facilitator: You mentioned that you sat around yesterday feeling sorry for yourself. Look at those words. Are those words, by themselves, the failure?

Matt: No.

Facilitator: Look at the picture (i.e., the memory) of you sitting around yesterday feeling sorry for yourself. Is that picture you?

Matt: I can see that it's a picture, but it feels like a failure. The sadness and contraction came up again.

Facilitator: Are the words "sadness and contraction" you, the failure?

Matt: No, those are just words.

Facilitator: Be aware of the sadness and contraction but without naming or labeling them. Is that energy you?

Matt: No, that's not me. But that energy feels stuck.

Facilitator: Whenever energy feels stuck in the body, that means there's still identification happening with our thoughts. Sometimes the thoughts appear as mental pictures instead of words. These mental pictures are being projected by the mind onto the sensation or emotion. Close your eyes and tell me if you see any mental pictures.

Matt: Yes, it feels like the energy is contained in a knot. I see a picture of the knot.

Facilitator: Look just at the picture of the knot by itself. Place no words on it. Gently observe the picture without describing it. Imagine it in a picture frame if that helps. Is that picture you, the failure?

Matt: No, I can see it's just a picture and it just relaxed. Now the sadness is welling up.

Facilitator: Relax all words and pictures and just experience that energy, letting it be exactly as it is. Take your time . . . Is that energy you?

Matt: Wow, no! It just moved through. I can see now that when no words or pictures are placed on emotion, it's not a failure. I don't feel like a failure.

Facilitator: Just rest in presence now, letting anything and everything arise and fall naturally. Can you find the self who's a failure?

Matt: I cannot find the failure. I see some faint words and pictures coming through but they feel light and empty. In fact, I cannot find a self. This is so simple and effective. And so freeing . . . I've literally been thinking of myself as something I cannot find when I really look.

Facilitator: Great! Whenever you find yourself telling the story that you're a failure, first try and rest in presence without emphasizing those thoughts. Feel the energy in the body without labeling it. If you still find yourself telling the story, try to find the failure using this inquiry.

Matt: I will. This is a great tool!

A Few Helpful Tips When Using the UI

Let's go back over the inquiry above and add some tips that may help as you begin doing this inquiry on your own. For the tips below, put yourself in place of Matt. When you do the inquiry on your own story, you might not choose "failure" as the thing you take yourself to be. Choose something that feels true for you.

Simplify thoughts down to either words or pictures.

If you look into your experience, you can see that thoughts arise in one of two different ways—words or pictures. Words are literally things like "Matt" or "I am a failure." Pictures are mental images that arise to awareness, such as the picture (i.e., memory) of sitting and feeling sorry for yourself or the picture of a body part or a knot. It's good to see the difference between words and pictures and to notice exactly which of these are arising to give you the sense of a separate self.

It may also be helpful to frame the particular words or pictures. For example, imagine the words "I'm miserable most of the time" inside a picture frame in your mind. Stare right at the content in the frame and then ask, "Is this me—the failure?" It may also be helpful to write the words down.

Refrain from trying to answer the question, "Is this it?" intellectually.

Notice that the facilitator requested Matt not to answer intellectually. Don't think about your answer. Don't analyze the question. Don't refer to other parts of your story to find the answer. Just look, presently, at one thought only. Look at the thought in the way you would look at a color without naming the color. Look directly, with thought-free observation. From that direct observation, ask, "Is this me—the failure?" Intellectually, you may see that this is just a thought, and not the object (failure). *But always pay attention to your body during the inquiry.* Notice when the body reacts with an emotion or sensation. This is the body's way of letting you know that, on some level, you believe that you're that thought. If the body reacts, answer "yes." If it doesn't react, answer "no."

Keep your answer to the question, "Is this me?" to a simple yes or no.

Don't add detailed analysis to the answer. For example, if you're truly a failure, and that failure is here, present in and as your body and mind, it shouldn't be hard to find. You should be able to find it right away, in your direct, present experience, without the need to elaborate. Take the example of looking for a pair of shoes in a closet. If you pick up a shirt, there's no need to give five reasons why the shirt isn't a pair of shoes. You know that it's not. No elaboration needed; you just keep looking for the shoes. Treat this inquiry the same way. Only stick to trying to find the object, with a simple yes or no.

Remember that you're looking for the object- not evidence of it, thoughts that point to it, or parts of it.

During the inquiry, it may seem as if every temporary thought, emotion, and sensation you encounter is "part of" the object, evidence of it, or pointing to it. Don't settle for this kind of thinking! Go deeper. *Look for the object itself.* If all these temporary things point to it, where are YOU—the real, permanent, separate, actual failure? If all words describe it, where are YOU? If these appearances are merely part of it, where are YOU? The YOU—the actual failure—is what you're looking for. And that's precisely what cannot be found when you do this inquiry.

For example, if you're looking for the failure you take yourself to be, it may seem as if the thought "I'm never going to succeed," is part of the failure. Forget about finding parts. Look for the failure itself. *Is the thought, "I'm never going to succeed" you—the actual failure?* That's the proper question. We often assume that these kinds of thoughts are describing or pointing to an actual, inherent failure that's *really there* under the thoughts. To prove that the failure isn't there under the thoughts, drop any thought that seems to describe or point to the failure. Notice that whenever you drop these thoughts, you can't find the failure. And, of course, you can't find it when the thoughts are there, either. You find only thoughts about a failure, one after the other—but no actual failure.

If you're looking at a thought and the thought seems to be the object, it always means that there's some sensation or emotion arising with the thought.

If the body reacts in any way to the question, "Is this thought me?" just say, "Yes, this is me." Then bring your thought-free attention immediately into the body and experience the emotion or sensation directly, letting it be exactly as it is, without trying to change or get rid of it. If you find your mind labeling the emotion or sensation with words such as "sadness" or "contraction," ask yourself, "Is the word 'sadness' me?" "Is the word 'contraction' me?" Then relax all thoughts for a few seconds, and experience the energy of the emotion or sensation, without any labels.

Simply sit with the raw sensory experience itself, resting in thought-free presence. And then ask, "Is this energy, by itself, me—the failure?" If you see that it's not the failure, let it be as it is, without trying to change or get rid of it. This frees up the energy to move and change naturally, often dissolving on its own. But the point isn't to try and get rid of or resist anything. That's just more seeking. The point is to see that the energy is *not* the failure. Once you see that no thought, emotion, or sensation is the object, it no longer matters whether these things arise. Any appearance can come and go, yet the failure is never found. This allows the story and emotions to quiet naturally and effortlessly. Suffering, seeking, and conflict show up in our experience as a result of unconsciously believing that these appearances form a separate object.

If an emotion or sensation in the body seems to be the object, it always means that there is a thought arising along with the sensation or emotion.

If this happens, observe the thought stream to see which thought (i.e., which words or pictures) is coming up with the sensation or emotion. Then look directly at that thought and ask, "Is this me?" An emotion or sensation only *seems* like the object when any identifying thought like "this is me" arises along with it.

Pay particular attention to the subtle mental pictures, such as images of body parts and other forms and shapes, which appear to contain certain emotions and sensations. If you see any pictures whenever you're experiencing emotions and sensations, ask whether that picture *is* the object. For example, is this picture of a knot *the* failure? As you begin to see that these are just mental images, and not the object, the pictures tend to change or disappear on their own. Even if they stick around, it won't matter much, once you see that they're, indeed, not the failure.

Once the words and pictures have dissolved around any emotion or sensation, remember to ask "Is this emotion, by itself, me—the failure?" or "Is this sensation, by itself, me—the failure?" and then let the emotion or sensation be as it is, without words or pictures. At that point, the energy will either stay, change or dissolve. Either way, this allows you to see that the energy is *just energy*. It's not a failure. Be careful to remember this step. In not remembering this step, you ignore bodily energy and keep the inquiries on a superficial or mental level only. Addiction is all about escaping or medicating bodily energies. Sitting with bodily energies, by themselves, and letting them be as they are is very helpful when it comes to releasing addiction. By including this step every time, we are essentially retraining our system to no longer escape or medicate these bodily energies.

When you are working with a facilitator, you may find that the facilitator refers to all emotions and sensations as "energies" or some other all-inclusive label. In this case, "energies" refers to *anything* felt in the body including emotions such as anger, sadness or fear as well as sensations such as tightness, pain, pleasure, or contraction. The facilitator is making no distinction between emotions and sensations. Putting all bodily energy into one category can help to simplify the process of looking. After all, when there are no labels on bodily energies, it's all just energy. Once simplified in this way, you can see that your entire experience is broken down into three categories (e.g., words, pictures, and energies) rather than the four categories previously discussed (words, pictures, sensations and emotions). You may also simplify your experience down to these three categories when doing the Living Inquiries on your own or you may break it down to words, pictures, sensations and emotions. Use whatever works best for you.

Undo the Velcro Effect

Whenever you think you're experiencing a separate object, notice that the thoughts, emotions, and sensations seem stuck together. That's the Velcro Effect. For example, when the thought, "I'm a failure" arises, it can feel as if sadness is stuck to the thought.

Really picking apart each thought, emotion, and sensation and then asking, "Is this me?" for each one is a powerful way of untangling the sense that thoughts, emotions, and sensations are stuck together. In seeing that no thought, emotion, or sensation is, by itself, the object, the Velcro Effect comes undone. The emptiness of the failure identity (or whatever object you're inquiring into) is now seen.

Once you do this inquiry a few times, you may no longer need to ask the question, "Is this me?" You may begin to see that this inquiry is just another way of pointing you to the direct experience of resting in presence and seeing that all energies arise and fall, never forming a separate object (e.g., a separate self).

Keep It Simple: Three Elements, One Question

Similar to the Compulsion Inquiry, you can keep the Unfindable Inquiry simple by remembering this: **three elements, one question.** For all the inquiries, there are only three elements to look at (words, pictures and energy). Energy includes both emotion and sensation. There is only one question stated in different ways:

"Are those words me, the victim?"

"Is that picture me, the victim?"

"Is this energy me, the victim?"

Keeping it that simple keeps the mind out of the game. This is a direct looking for a self or other thing.

Using the Unfindable Inquiry on Addictive Substances and Activities

You can use the Unfindable Inquiry on anything to which you feel addicted (e.g., a drug, a glass of wine, a casino, the Internet). Addiction is all about separation. Separation creates the sense that there's a separate person, here, who must indulge in a separate object, out there. Using the UI on substances and activities helps the mind withdraw from fixation on the addictive substance or activity itself.

Let's say your substance of choice is a martini. Each day, around 5:00 pm, you begin craving a martini. You find your body unconsciously moving to the kitchen and your hands pulling out the glass and making the martini. You drink one after the other, until you fall asleep or pass out. This is like being asleep to your desire for the drink, as if on autopilot.

Now let's take a look at that entire sequence from another angle. Using the UI, you begin to wake up in the midst of the desire itself by trying to find the object (martini) in words, pictures and bodily energies.

The moment you have the thought, "I want a martini," rest in presence and look directly at the words. Ask: "Are those words, by themselves, the martini?" If your response is "no," you can just keep looking for the martini in whatever words, pictures and energies that arise. But if your response is "yes," notice that energy (i.e., some emotion or sensation) is arising in the body along with those words.

Now relax and bring thought-free attention to the sensation or emotion. Maybe it's a craving or anxiety. Rest and experience the sensation without the words, "I want a martini," and without all other words and pictures. Is that sensation itself the martini when you aren't labeling it? Notice it as nameless energy. This energy, when you aren't adding words and pictures to it, comes and goes. It relaxes. Yet, even if it doesn't relax, you can see that the energy isn't the martini. Remember: If any emotion or sensation feels like the object, it means there's a thought arising. Look at the thought and see that it's not the martini.

Taking brief moments of relaxing in thought-free presence, in-between the questions, helps a lot during this inquiry. Notice that, during the few seconds of relaxing without thoughts, nothing is needed. In that moment, life is complete just as it is. Sensations and emotions may be coming through, but for a few seconds, at least, they aren't hooking into any stories about desiring a martini.

As you're resting, look again for the martini in the next words, pictures or energies that arise. Don't actively make thoughts appear. Just relax and notice when they arise naturally and then look again. Maybe this time, you see a mental picture of the bottle sitting inside the cabinet. Look directly at that mental picture. Ask yourself, "Is that picture *it*?" Notice that it's just a picture. Let the picture change or relax on its own, once you see it for what it is.

Notice that you cannot find the martini in any individual words, pictures, or energies, no matter how thoroughly you look. Even if you end up grabbing a martini, look to see if the color or texture of the bottle, or any other sensation of taste or smell, by itself, is the martini. None of those energies, by themselves, are the martini.

A martini never "calls your name." It doesn't contain any magnetic pull on its own. One person can become addicted to martinis while another person can feel repulsed by them. The magnetic pull is an illusion created by misperceiving your experience. A martini doesn't exist solely on its own accord. The martini craving arises by way of thoughts, emotions, and sensations that seem welded together. The mind creates an association between well-being and what it perceives as the source of that well-being—a martini. This misperception results in the brain's pleasure center being hijacked, creating a repetitive urge to drink, over and over each night. Interrupt that association by using this inquiry each time you feel the urge to drink.

During the inquiry, as you move back and forth between words, pictures or energies (one by one), these appearances feel less and less welded together. The words and mental pictures of the martini start to feel weaker. They begin to dissolve more quickly each time you look at them. The emotions and sensations that arise with these thoughts are more easily experienced without labels.

This makes the object of your desire appear emptier and more transparent in your perception. You're able to witness the words and pictures more, instead of unconsciously following the trail of these thoughts like a straight line to the vodka bottle. You discover that what you were seeing in your mind as a martini calling your name is more like a movie. Yet, now the movie is conscious. You're no longer asleep in the desire. It's now easier to rest in presence. In that restfulness, you're seeing through the sense of separation that lies at the heart of addiction.

Instead of doing the UI on the martini, you can do it on "the person who desires a martini." Try to find yourself. Is the thought "I want a martini" you? No, it's just a thought. How about the mental image of you drinking a martini later in the day, is that you, the person that desires a martini? No, it's just a picture. How about the craving in your chest or stomach when you don't label it? Is that you—the person who wants a martini? No, it's just nameless energy.

The Unfindable Inquiry is similar to the SNoRRe method. Both are designed to help you rest more fully in presence—noticing words, pictures and bodily energies but without emphasizing them. If either method seems too difficult or cumbersome, stick to the simple practice of resting in thought-free presence, over and over, whenever addictive thoughts arise. Use whatever works! That's the key.

The Boomerang Inquiry (Finding Harmony in Relationships)

The Core Deficient Self—A Believable Illusion

Most people carry a deficiency story that strikes at the very heart of who they think they are. It's the core story of the self-center. This core story is some version of "there is something wrong with me." It comes in many forms: "I'm unlovable," "I'm not good enough," "I'm lacking," "I'm incomplete," "I'm not 'there' yet," "I'm wrong," "I'm weak," "I'm unsafe," "I'm insecure," "I'm imperfect," or "I'm inadequate." And that's just the short list. The form it takes is unique to every individual.

The core deficient self is a false script about ourselves that we carry around in life, from childhood into adulthood. It's an offshoot of a belief in being separate. There really isn't a core deficient, separate self. We just believe there is. We're carrying around a fundamental lie about who we really are. There's a palpable emotional aspect to this lie, a wound that gets triggered when other people seem to mirror this story back to us. This lie hurts. It's responsible for much of the difficulty we experience in relationships.

Relationship Is a Mirror

Relationship has a built-in mirroring effect. As we move through life, other people appear to reflect back to us this core, deficient self. When this sense of deficiency is triggered in relationship, an emotional wound arises. If the pain seems like too much, we may find ourselves trying to avoid it, blame others for it, or medicate it somehow by reaching for addictive substances or activities. There's a tendency to focus our attention outward toward others, as if they're the source of the pain. But others are just a mirror showing us what we believe about ourselves. Here are a few signs indicating that we're carrying a belief in self-deficiency:

Insisting on being right and making others wrong

Seeking love, praise, attention, acknowledgment, or approval

Comparing ourselves to others as better or worse

Belittling, ridiculing, or bullying others

Trying to control or manipulate others

Judging others negatively or complaining about them

Alienating ourselves and avoiding certain painful relationships

Acting on selfish ambition

Feeling jealous or envious of others

Much of this mind activity is based in fear of looking directly at who we've falsely taken *ourselves* to be—deficient in some way. The others in our lives are constantly mirroring this illusion of self back to us.

If you look, the mirroring effect is happening in every direction. The view of others as successful often mirrors back an "unsuccessful self." When a loved one doesn't respond to you the way you expected, or a romantic relationship ends, this often mirrors back an "unlovable self." Attractive people may mirror back an "unattractive self." People who look important in the world may mirror back an "unimportant self" or "unworthy self." When someone judges or criticizes you, this may mirror back a self that feels wrong. When others appear arrogant or authoritative, this may reflect back a weak, insignificant or small self. If others appear powerful, you may feel less powerful or powerless.

It's not just other people. Anything can reflect deficiency back to you. An addiction to a drug or some other thing mirrors back a self that's lacking or "not enough." Future things such as enlightenment, recovery, and self-improvement may point back to a self that seems presently incomplete.

The Boomerang Inquiry adds an additional step to the Unfindable Inquiry (UI) and we use it on the core deficiency story as it shows up in relationship.

Like a boomerang that returns back to the thrower, the deficient self is reflected back to you in relationship. The Boomerang Inquiry focuses on seeing that mirroring effect and then, with the UI, seeing through the deficient self that's being mirrored or reflected back. The relationship could be with anything— any person, place, event, goal, or other thing. When we really believe that we're deficient at the core, almost everything in our lives can appear to confirm this story.

Here's how the Boomerang Inquiry works:

1. *Use the mirror.* Whenever you're triggered in relationship, find out what deficiency story this person or thing is mirroring back to you.

2. *Name it.* Give the deficient self *a specific name* (e.g., unlovable self, unfulfilled self, lacking self, incomplete self, broken self, unsuccessful self, unsafe self, invalid self, etc.). Whatever you pick, make sure it feels true for you, as if that is what you really are at the core.

3. *Find it.* Once you name that deficient self, *try to find it* using the UI.

You can see that the Boomerang Inquiry is very similar to the Unfindable Inquiry. Steps 2 and 3 are the same "name it, find it" elements from the UI. *The Boomerang Inquiry simply adds a new first step—using the mirror of relationship to identify the core deficiency story that is being triggered within you in a particular relationship scenario.* The Boomerang Inquiry applies whenever you're looking at how something outside yourself (e.g. another person, object or situation) seems to make you feel deficient in some way.

An Example of the Boomerang Inquiry

Tricia: My husband, Brian, triggers me almost every day. I catch him looking at other women. I notice that he doesn't listen to me and this really bothers me. I've tried talking to him about emotions, but he can't talk about that. He says I'm overreacting to everything.

Facilitator: In those moments when you catch him looking at other women, what does that mirror back to you about being deficient?

Tricia: Ugly. I feel like I'm not good enough for him.

Facilitator: How about the times when he isn't listening to you or doesn't want to talk about the things you wish to talk about?

Tricia: I feel as if he's shutting me out and that hurts.

Facilitator: Now name the deficient self. If you could reduce that whole story about how he makes you feel to one specific kind of deficient self, what would it be? Reduce it down to something that really feels like you at the core.

Tricia: I'm not loved. That sums it up completely.

Facilitator: Now find it. Try to find that unloved self. Relax and just notice the capacity to be aware of thoughts coming and going. Look right at the words "I'm not loved." Are those words you—the unloved self? If it helps, you can imagine putting those words in a picture frame in your mind, to really isolate them so you can look directly at them.

Tricia: Let me take a moment. Are the words "I'm not loved" me? Yes, that's me. That's how I feel about myself.

Facilitator: When words feel like who you are, it just means some emotion or sensation is arising along with the words. The words feel stuck to the emotion or sensation. That's the Velcro Effect. Take a moment, bring attention into your body, and see what emotion or sensation is arising.

Tricia: Sadness.

Facilitator: Look right at the word, "sadness." Imagine the word in a picture frame. Is that you—the unloved self?

Tricia: No, that's clearly just a word.

Facilitator: Let that word fall away and bring attention back into your body. Can you feel the energy that you're calling sadness? Not the word sadness, but the actual energy in your body?

Tricia: Yes.

Facilitator: Take a moment and just notice that you're presently aware of that energy, without a name for it. Gently observe that energy. Is that energy you—the unloved person?

Tricia: Yes, that's me.

Facilitator: Whenever an emotion or sensation feels like you, it just means there are some words or mental pictures arising along with it. If you just take a moment and look into your mind, watching thoughts, what words or pictures are arising along with that energy?

Tricia: The words "I've always had this problem with men."

Facilitator: Look right at those words. Are those words you—the unloved self?

Tricia: Those are just words. When I looked at them, they fell away.

Facilitator: Bring attention back into your body. Do you feel that energy still?

Tricia: Yes.

Facilitator: Look again at that energy, without labeling it. Just let all words and pictures come to rest. Observe. Is that energy, by itself, you?

Tricia: No, that's just energy. And it dissolved as soon as those words dissolved.

Facilitator: Bring up a memory of the last time Brian wasn't listening to you and you felt hurt.

Tricia: That's not hard. He did it this morning.

Facilitator: Look directly at that mental picture of you talking this morning, while he's not listening. Frame it, if that helps. Is that picture you?

Tricia: No, that's just a memory. It's not me.

Facilitator: Look at the words, "He looks at other women." Are those words you—the unloved person? Stick to yes or no. Don't elaborate.

Tricia: No.

Facilitator: How about "He doesn't listen to me and this bothers me?"

Tricia: No.

Facilitator: Just be in presence for a few seconds, scanning the space of your inner body. Let any thought, emotion, or sensation arise naturally. Where's the unloved person? Can you find it?

Tricia: I don't know what you mean.

Facilitator: You've come to me saying that you're an unloved person. I assume that this is who you've taken yourself to be for many years, right?

Tricia: Yes, since childhood.

Facilitator: If this is really who you are, shouldn't you be able to find that right now? When a child is looking for an Easter egg she isn't ambivalent about what she's looking for. Either she spots it or she doesn't. If there's an unloved person sitting with me here right now, can you point me to it?

Tricia: Yes, it's me.

Facilitator: Are the words, "Yes, it's me" the unloved self?

Tricia: <laughing> No! Just words.

Facilitator: Look for the unloved person.

Tricia: It seems to be in my name.

Facilitator: Look directly and only at the word "Tricia." Is that the unloved person?

Tricia: No, but it seems to point to her.

Facilitator: Find the unloved person that's right here. Not just words pointing to her. Find HER.

Tricia: I can't. Wait, yes, I can. I see the thought, "I know he loves me but I don't feel it."

Facilitator: Are those words you, the unloved person? Don't think about the words or add more words to them. Just look directly at those words and answer.

Tricia: Well, intellectually, I know they're just words. But there's sadness arising again.

Facilitator: Whenever the body reacts to the words, just say "yes." Bring your attention into the body to feel that energy without words and pictures. Is that energy you?

Tricia: No. The energy is relaxing now. It actually feels very warm and loving. I cannot find the unloved me at all. I'm now just sitting here in peace, feeling totally free of that story. I can see the memory of my dad now though. He was cold. But when I look right at that picture, I can see it's not me, the unloved person. Wait, there's a picture in my mind of me as a ten-year-old girl. That's the unloved me.

Facilitator: Is that picture of the girl you, the unloved self?

Tricia: I can see it's just a picture. I went straight into the body to feel the energy of sadness and it washed through. No, it's not me. Wow, I've been in this story for a long time. I can't find her, the unloved self.

Facilitator: Take a look at Brian again in your mind. Does the sense that you're an unloved person arise when you look at him? Is the boomerang at work again?

Tricia: No, he looks perfect just as he is. I can see I love him. Actually, it's more than that. It's just love. I don't feel like it's missing. This was just a story I was placing on him. Thank you, thank you. This is as clear as day now. I feel so much lighter!

Facilitator: Yes, and when the story is "I'm unloved," we believe others contain our love, withholding it from us.

Tricia: What a cruel joke!

This is called the Boomerang Inquiry because we bring these core deficient stories to relationships. Like a boomerang, Tricia sent the message out that she feels like an unloved person. She played the part, spoke the language of an unloved person, and reacted to Brian from that belief about herself. Brian's actions were then interpreted by Tricia as unloving. Whether Brian's actions were objectively unloving makes no difference to Tricia's story. The interpretation was happening in Tricia's mind— in words, pictures, emotions, and sensations. The boomerang of "I'm unloved" came right back to Tricia.

There's an unconscious drive within us to attract people and situations and to interpret the actions of others in a way that confirms this core deficiency story. We solidify these stories over and over, like a pattern that repeats itself in all relationships, until that deficient self is seen through. Tricia was never a deficient person. There are no deficient people, just old scripts running.

Notice that, near the end, the facilitator asked Tricia to look again at Brian, once she couldn't find the unloved person. When she looked at him, she no longer felt that trigger. The deficient self did not arise. And so the interpretation of "I'm an unloved person" was no longer operating. The boomerang did not return.

Love feels natural once we stop telling the story, "I am a separate, unloved person." Relationships automatically harmonize themselves once the deficient self is seen as unfindable. This doesn't mean we must stay in every relationship. We either stay or leave. The right action to take becomes clearer once we're no longer looking at others through the lens of a deficient self.

For a more in-depth view of the Boomerang Inquiry and how to use it in all relationships, refer to www.livinginquiries.com.

CHAPTER EIGHT: Natural Rest Groups

The Formation of Groups

Natural Rest Groups can be a powerful mechanism for mutual support in recovery. Mutual support of each other, especially in the beginning of recovery, is beneficial.

Some may not feel comfortable being involved with a group. They may choose to work on their own. This isn't recommended. If this is your choice, it's suggested that you find support with at least one other person involved with this way of recovery.

Natural Rest Group meetings may take place online or in a local community. A meeting is any gathering of two or more who come together for the purpose of supporting one another in this way of recovery.

This chapter is meant only as a general guideline or set of suggestions. Natural Rest Groups have autonomy. They govern themselves.

Groups may take donations during meetings in order to be fully self-supporting and to pay rent for the facility in which the meeting takes place as well as any other costs associated with meetings.

Natural Rest Groups and meetings should center on the practices in this book. They should provide those attending with information on how to find this book and any other online or written literature on this topic.

Servants

The group as a whole may designate certain people to act as servants. Servants make themselves available to support those who are struggling with resting in presence.

In order to be a servant, a person should have direct experience with the benefits of restful presence as well as shadow work, perspective taking, and the inquiries.

Servants should, at all times, refrain from imposing their viewpoints on others. To be a servant is to be of service to others, not to teach or preach to others.

Being a servant isn't about being special in the eyes of others.

A servant's function is to serve with selflessness, honesty, integrity, compassion, and humility, without a desire for attention, praise, or acknowledgment. This selflessness, of course, is naturally available in presence.

A servant never seeks a return on his or her investment in any relationship. He or she gives without the expectation of any particular result.

Servants are mindful that people are in different places in their practice of resting in presence, shadow work, perspective taking, and the inquiries in this book. A suggestion for one person might not be helpful for another. Servants meet people where they are.

Natural Rest Groups may also designate servants with specific skills to run meetings, take care of group money, and perform other administrative duties. Servants aren't in charge of the group. They have no authority. The group as a whole has the authority. All actions should be taken from the perspective of what's beneficial for everyone involved.

Servants may also act as mentors in one-on-one relationships. Those who are new to this way of recovery may need direct guidance and help in the beginning. They can request a servant to act as a mentor.

Servants can share their direct experience with resting in presence, and help with inquiries, shadow work, and perspective taking in these one-on-one relationships.

The function of these relationships isn't to identify with roles such as newcomer, servant, and mentor. We're not any of these conceptual labels. The purpose of these relationships is to support each other in directly experiencing the benefits of restful presence.

Servants may have experience facilitating the Compulsion, Unfindable and Boomerang Inquiries for others. But servants are not necessarily formally trained as facilitators.

There are people available who are formally trained as facilitators and who work over the phone and the internet with others. Again, it is important to work with a trained facilitator or— at the very least—someone with a lot of experience with these particular inquiries, before trying them on your own.

About Natural Rest Meetings

A meeting may consist of quiet time at the beginning or end of the meeting and/or sharing among members.

During the meeting, people are encouraged to share their own experience with resting in presence and how that benefits them in recovery.

The group may split off into smaller groups or one-on-one sessions to do shadow work or other inquiries in this book.

All newcomers and those who've relapsed are welcomed into the meetings with open arms, without judgment or condemnation.

It's important for newcomers and those who've relapsed to hear that relaxing repeatedly into the natural rest of presence is working for others.

Clean and sober time or years of recovery may be celebrated. But all members of Natural Rest Groups are considered equal, regardless of clean time or years of recovery.

A woman who's suffered a heroin addiction is equal to a man who's suffered a sweet tooth addiction.

A person who's been court-ordered into a meeting after committing a crime is equal to a wealthy housewife with a shopping addiction.

We value those who have years of experience with resting in presence. We listen to their experience and ask for their support and guidance.

But emphasizing these conceptual labels, such as newcomer, relapser, servant, heroin addict, criminal, and housewife, tends to keep us feeling separate from one another. It keeps us locked into the pattern of self-centeredness including self-loathing or self-righteousness. It plays into the false sense of deficiency or lack that so many have carried around since childhood. That sense of deficiency or lack lies at the core of our addiction. Encouraging that kind of thinking in the group setting can lead people to relapse.

All we really have is the present moment. A moment of restful presence is more valuable to us in our recovery than emphasizing clean time, roles, identities, personal histories, and war stories.

Although we value those who've had many years of experience staying clean, our recovery isn't ultimately judged by the number of years we've been clean or the particular addictive substances we've used or activities in which we've engaged.

The true value of our recovery lies in our willingness to rest in presence in any moment in which we find ourselves seeking and to provide mutual support to each other.

We mutually support each other for the purpose of remaining clean and sober from our favorite addictive substances and activities, avoiding relapse and finding freedom from addictive seeking in all areas of our lives.

Some within the group may not be able to refrain totally from their particular addictive substance or activity. For example, food is necessary to life. Those suffering from food addiction cannot stop eating. Similarly, workaholics may not be able to stop working completely.

Resting in presence is beneficial for everyone, including those suffering from food and work addictions.

We're sensitive to the fact that some people cannot totally abstain from these substances and activities. They should not be made to feel different.

We want to support those who must find a way to moderate rather than refrain totally from their addictive substance or activity in such areas of food and work.

Avoiding Excessive Storytelling

Everyone is encouraged to share his or her direct experience openly in Natural Rest Group meetings. Sometimes, hearing someone tell his or her story helps us all to see we are not alone in our pain. However, we avoid *excessive* personal storytelling for important reasons.

We avoid emphasizing views within a time-bound story like, "I'm destined to be an addict all my life," "I will never drink again," or "My past keeps me from being present."

Belief in these views reinforces the thought-based, time-bound story of "me." They reinforce self-centeredness. They place us in conceptual boxes.

When we live from within these conceptual boxes, we're focused mainly on ourselves. We cannot truly listen to other people.

We tend to carry these time-bound stories with us, wherever we go. We tend to repeat them, as if they're real, rather than just stories we tell ourselves.

It may be helpful to let people know how we're feeling, especially when we're suffering or seeking.

It may be helpful to share in a meeting about recent past events or something coming up in the future, if such sharing helps us to see where we're emphasizing the story instead of resting in presence.

But as we rest more and more in presence, and experience the unmistakable benefits of presence for ourselves, we find that excessive personal storytelling is often a way to avoid actually feeling the emotions that are driving the stories.

When we're telling our stories repeatedly and excessively, often we're not noticing the self-centeredness in them. Emphasizing storytelling, rather than resting in presence, can solidify the self-center, keeping the cycle of addiction alive.

We share personal stories during group meetings mainly just to illuminate how resting in presence helps free us from identifying with these stories.

When we're experiencing difficulty with resting in presence, we look to servants and others within the group who can provide direct support and experience.

We may break off into smaller groups or into one-on-one sessions to do shadow work and perspective taking, to seek advice from servants, or to share about highly personal issues for which we need support.

If we're ever on the verge of relapse, we're encouraged to speak openly about that, either during a meeting or afterwards to a servant or a friend or family member. We're encouraged to let others know so that we can find support. We never keep thoughts of relapse private.

Relapse can happen. Sometimes we are lulled into a false sense of security, believing that a long period of time—even years—resting in presence somehow immunizes us from falling back into an addictive pattern once we pick up a substance or activity again. But presence is not a long term insurance plan against relapse. *It is not about time at all!* Time is always a story. The story is the very self-centeredness we see through in this way of recovery.

Presence is a *timeless* restfulness that is always with us. We come to experience this directly. However, certain chemicals are released in the brain when we return to addictive substances and activities. The brain's pleasure center can easily be hijacked once again, recreating a pattern of addiction. The key to releasing the addictive cycle is not found through mental certainty or telling a time-bound personal story that we are beyond all addictions. It's about rest in the present moment. It's about the openness to see through our self-centered stories as they arise and allow all energies, including cravings and uncomfortable emotions, to be as they are.

Letting others know about our own desire to relapse helps us illuminate the stories behind that desire. Others can help us see what we cannot see. We can easily blind ourselves to the emotions that we are trying to avoid or cover up. Often, the desire to relapse comes from an inner sense of deficiency or lack. The Unfindable and Boomerang Inquiries can come in handy during these times.

Confidentiality and Anonymity

All meetings are confidential. We never share with anyone outside the group the names of members of the group or anything discussed during meetings.

Confidentiality and anonymity are of utmost importance in providing a safe and secure place where we can mutually support each other in gaining experiential certainty about the benefits of presence.

Conflict

We avoid overindulging in political, religious, philosophical, scientific and intellectual viewpoints during the meetings.

We emphasize only the importance and benefit of resting in presence in all situations.

We share with each other about how resting in presence has released us from feeling strongly attached to these divisive viewpoints.

Viewpoints will always appear. We respect all viewpoints as they appear. We celebrate diversity with regard to age, race, gender, sexual orientation, nationality, religion, political affiliation, and all other areas.

This isn't a method in which we're trying to eliminate viewpoints. We're simply providing an atmosphere where relaxing into restful presence is our common ground.

During meetings, we don't turn "rest" into an intellectual viewpoint, which we impose upon others. Rest isn't a sword that we wield in some attempt to control or change others.

We make the decision personally to rest in presence.

This is the most important decision we can make in our recovery.

This decision transforms us.

We find no need to impose any viewpoint on anyone. We feel free to share our viewpoint but always with humility and respect for others. This is not something we *try* to do. This way of interacting becomes natural as we rely more on presence, and less on thoughts for a sense of self.

Humility and respect happen automatically through presence.

As we see through identification with thought, we may find an even greater capacity to express ourselves, but without having to defend or protect a self and without having to make enemies out of those who disagree.

Perspective Taking During Meetings

During meetings and in our relationships, we take the perspective of every person sharing. We don't listen for the purpose of agreeing or disagreeing only. We listen without judgment and allow the person's words to create his or her story in our minds.

We feel into the person's perspective completely. This reveals that the boundary between self and other is a conceptual boundary only.

Only our stories divide us.

When we take the perspective of the one who's speaking during a meeting, the boundary is no longer there.

All that's left is nonjudgmental presence listening openly to whatever story is appearing within its space.

This space of presence is love itself. It can be trusted completely. The meetings become an atmosphere of unconditional love.

By really listening to each other, we're gaining insight about different perspectives in the world. We're seeing life from the eyes of others.

Through selfless listening and perspective taking, a compassionate response to others comes automatically. We may eventually agree or disagree with someone's viewpoint or behavior, especially if it's harmful to others or us. But our first priority in all communications is to take the perspective of the other person to the best of our ability.

Unconditional love seeks only to be of selfless service to others, to provide experience, advice, or direction when it's needed or requested, always with complete humility, compassion, and respect.

Meetings become a source of incredible insight and mutual support. They provide an atmosphere where our relationships can deepen.

Shadows in Meetings

In meetings or any other situation in which we're in the company of others, shadows may arise.

One of the most common shadows in meetings may be the self-centeredness shadow.

As someone is sharing his or her struggle during a meeting, we may feel a tendency to judge him or her as self-centered. Fair enough! The person sharing may indeed be locked in a self-centered story.

But the more another person's self-centeredness really gets under our skin, the more likely we're shadow boxing.

When we repress the trait of self-centeredness within us, it starts to appear "out there" in everyone else.

Presence isn't about repressing or denying anything. It's about bringing each aspect of our own self-centered story into the light of present awareness.

When we find ourselves shadow boxing others who are "self-centered" in the meetings or in other areas of our lives, we can do the 3–2–1 shadow process.

In re-owning the shadow, we see that we've repressed our own self-centeredness.

After all, what's self-centeredness? Isn't self-centeredness the thought process that places the self at the center of life?

In the moment of being fixated on someone else's self-centeredness, you place yourself at the center of life, and think of yourself as someone who's transcended self-centeredness. This sense of being someone who is special or better is self-*centered* thinking.

The story "I am not self-centered but others are" is a story that separates us from each other.

As with all shadow work, the point isn't to re-own the story of being self-centered and then begin believing that story. We're not any of these conceptual stories.

We let self-centered thoughts arise completely and fully. When they do arise, we simply don't emphasize them. In this way, we aren't trying to repress stories. Repression tends to lead to shadow boxing.

We may also find ourselves shadow hugging servants or others who we perceive to be wise, selfless, or spiritually awakened. It's fine to look to others for guidance and support. However, the more the positive traits of others really attract us, the more likely we're shadow hugging.

When we shadow hug others, we're repressing our own natural truth, beauty, love, wisdom, and selflessness. We're pretending that selfless presence isn't available to us. We're projecting it outward onto others.

Through the 3–2–1 process, we re-own these positive stories we've projected onto others.

We come to see all positive and negative stories and energies to be equal movements of presence. They're all allowed to be exactly as they are, but we don't rely on any of them for a sense of self.

Through re-owning shadows and resting in presence, we realize that the selfless presence we were idealizing in another is also our own true nature.

Working with Each Other and Other Groups

We find that restful presence, coupled with shadow work, perspective taking, and the inquiries in this book, allow us to open up to each other within the group and allow our group to be open to other groups that serve a different purpose or present a different perspective.

We work with other organizations to the extent that they don't jeopardize our purpose, which is to provide a safe, confidential place where we can mutually support each other and share our direct experience of finding recovery through presence.

When we work with other groups, we want to maintain the integrity, confidentiality, and structure of our Natural Rest Groups and meetings.

We want to avoid conflict with other groups and viewpoints. We do this by simply resting in presence when we work with others. We rest when we notice the appearance of the viewpoint that "only our group is right."

Group-centered thinking like this is similar to self-centered thinking.

In Natural Rest Groups, we're not seeking a personal or collective identity as a "Natural Rest Member." We're only sharing our experience with finding recovery through restful presence.

Self-centered and group-centered viewpoints and identities create the appearance of boundaries that aren't ultimately here. These boundaries are found in thought only.

Conflict and division that results from treating these boundaries as being real may interfere with our capacity to use this way of recovery in the most beneficial way, to mutually support others, and to work with other groups.

Whenever we're defending a viewpoint or comparing ourselves to others, we're creating boundary lines. All boundary lines are potential battle lines.

We find that selfless presence brings forth a natural desire to be engaged with life on every level, including in our close personal relationships and also with other groups and entities such as churches, other recovery programs, rehabilitation centers, and courts within our communities.

We find that these various systems, groups, and entities can work together. We find that we all have a common goal, which is to heal the destruction that addiction has left in our lives and in the lives of our families and communities.

We find that responding to others through compassion happens automatically. In selfless presence, we want to be involved with important causes that benefit all sentient beings.

Presence reveals a bottomless depth of selflessness and creative potential. Service doesn't feel like an obligation. It's a natural attribute of presence.

In presence, we live in abundance. We're no longer taking and seeking. We experience a natural and automatic desire to give and to work with others inside and outside the group.

Presence has a profound sense of love within it. We experience a deep connection with each other in the stillness and peace of the present moment.

This love transcends the conceptual boundaries we impose upon each other in our stories. The line between me vs. you and us vs. them becomes transparent.

We find that, when we rest in presence, instead of emphasizing stories about each other and ourselves, this love deepens. Unconditional love is realized when these conceptual boundaries are seen through.

In the undivided, loving, no-boundary space of the present moment, we're open to and compassionate with each other. We heal together—personally, and in our relationships, families, and communities. To find a Natural Rest Group in your area or to form your own group, visit www.naturalrestforaddiction.com.

CHAPTER NINE: Physical Health

Our Holistic view of Recovery

This book is a holistic way of recovery. We're concerned with total well-being in every facet of life. In previous chapters, we spoke of the mental and emotional well-being that we discover through the simple practice of relaxing repeatedly into the natural rest of presence.

We've also addressed the harmony and well-being found in relationships through presence as well as when we make perspective taking and shadow work important in our lives.

We've addressed the importance of meeting in groups to provide mutual support for each other as well as the importance of involvement with our families and communities.

We see that our present experience includes all these perspectives—mental, emotional, spiritual, and relational. By repeatedly relaxing into present moment awareness, these perspectives become clearer for us. They all come *naturally* into view.

By resting, we don't have to make an *effort* to take care of ourselves in these areas. We find that these areas take care of themselves. All we have to do is rest in presence in all situations, and remain open to learn from others who have direct experience of the benefits of presence.

Perspective on Physical Health

Our present experience also includes a physical component. We find that resting in presence makes it easier for us to take care of our bodies.

By repeatedly relaxing into present awareness, the stress and fear about our bodies can relax.

We no longer cling to self-images of being attractive or unattractive, heavy or thin, young or old, healthy or sick. These images have been propelling us into the future. We've been chasing a better image of ourselves. This is just another form of seeking.

These images may still arise in presence, but they lose the power to control us or make us feel bad about ourselves.

The solution is always very simple: rest in presence whenever we notice that we're emphasizing past or future mental images of ourselves.

As each thought is allowed to come and go, we simply rest as the space of the present moment. Recognizing presence releases the stress and fear around the future and around the mental viewpoints involving our bodies, our health, and our ages.

A Different Way

In presence, we find that we want to take care of our bodies for a different reason. Instead of chasing some future mental image based in the vanity of ego or the fear of sickness and death, we become interested in present health and physical well-being for its own sake. We identify less with thoughts about our bodies and the sensations that arise and fall. Our bodies are not what we are ultimately, yet they appear as a precious, present resource.

We may find that nutritional plans, exercise programs, and other techniques and methods for the well-being of the mind and body can be beneficial additions to the practices in this book. For example, those suffering from food addiction may find that excess sugar and other foods create cravings. It may be helpful to cut out or decrease our intake of certain foods that create cravings, make us feel tired, or affect our emotional well-being.

We begin to see our bodies more clearly, without the fog of fear and anxiety about the future and also without the distorted, self-defeating images of our bodies carried over from the past.

In the present moment, we begin to experience our bodies in a different way. We see that "body" can be accounted for entirely through words, pictures and energy.

Through repeatedly relaxing into the natural rest of presence, our bodies begin to feel lighter, more transparent.

What we took to be a body is experienced as a sensation here and a sensation there, along with certain words and pictures arising about a body. There's no body to be found beyond these words, pictures and energy. If this seems unclear in your experience, working with a facilitator who can guide you through the Unfindable Inquiry will help a lot.

These words, pictures and energies are appearing directly within present awareness. Identification with the body as a solid and separate object drops away in this realization. We can relax into the spacious, natural rest of presence. In this presence, we feel good about being alive. There's a natural well-being and desire to take care of our bodies. They aren't who we are, but they appear and deserve attention.

Illness

In recognizing that our true body is awareness itself, we're keenly aware and alert to what's happening within us. We're no longer lost in mental stories about our bodies.

We notice discomfort, pain, and other symptoms the moment they arise. We relax from the tendency to emphasize stressful and fearful thoughts around any discomfort, pain, or symptoms.

We no longer have to remain afraid of suffering and illness. Clinging to fearful thoughts about future physical suffering is self-centeredness.

In emphasizing thoughts of future impending doom and illness, instead of resting in presence, we stay locked in fear. This fear becomes an obstacle to taking present, healthy action that benefits us physically.

We notice that stressful and fearful thoughts don't help us take care of ourselves. They only paralyze us. What helps us take care of ourselves is attending to our present physical needs, which means eating right, getting a good night's sleep, and visiting proper nutritionists and health care professionals when necessary.

These are practical steps we can take in the present moment. They don't involve incessant thinking about future doom. They don't involve emphasizing conceptual labels like "sick person" or "addict."

Presence may not get rid of physical pain. But in resting in presence through periods of chronic or intense physical pain, the mental and emotional suffering around the pain can relax.

We notice any mental or emotional resistance to physical pain, symptoms, or discomforts. Noticing resistance naturally allows the pain, symptom, or discomfort to be as it is.

Through presence, the resistance falls away. All that's left is the present pain, symptom, or discomfort. We can deal with this. It's the suffering that overwhelms us.

To suffer means, "to carry over in time." It means to resist and then make a time-bound story out of the pain, symptom, or discomfort.

All we ever have to deal with is what's happening now.

The story, "I've been suffering in physical pain for years" and the story, "I'll probably suffer physically for many more years" are nothing more than presently arising thoughts. They're just stories. Through resting in presence, we see them for what they are. We let these stories of resistance come to rest.

We see that all we ever have to deal with is a present sensation of pain. We no longer have to emphasize the story of suffering in the past or future. Yesterday's pain is not happening now. Tomorrow's pain is nowhere to be found. This releases the layer of storytelling around the present sensation of pain.

The storytelling causes us to suffer unnecessarily. It adds a sort of mental and emotional layer over the pain. It's much easier to cope with a present sensation than to cope with a story of having suffered for years.

In being presently alert to what's happening within us, without emphasizing self-centered, fearful story lines and labels, we're better able to take effective action that benefits our physical health.

We may find that certain foods, exercise, and proper sleep provide benefit to us. We share this information with each other in meetings.

Relaxing into the present moment allows us to visit the doctor or even be admitted into the hospital in a state of emotional and mental rest and well-being. Fear is no longer running the show.

If fear arises as we visit the doctor or hospital, we allow it to be just as it is. It comes and goes as a movement of presence itself. In presence, fear isn't resisted. It's allowed to be. It cannot touch our ultimate, real identity as presence.

No label can touch our ultimate identity as presence either. If we're diagnosed with an illness, we don't have to live within that label. We don't have to emphasize the label, "I'm a cancer patient," or "I'm a diabetic." We don't have to treat other people as if they're these stories either.

In letting these labels and stories come to rest, we can simply be what we are, presence itself. Presence cannot be contained within any conceptual box.

Even in times of extreme physical illness and pain, we find the restful nature of presence continues to shine radiantly and uninterruptedly.

The sacredness and stillness of presence carries us through the most challenging times. It's our constant companion. We can rely on this presence in every situation, regardless of our physical state.

We find we can take care of ourselves perfectly without emphasizing self-centered stories and labels about being sick or being a dying person.

The Unfindable and Boomerang Inquiries are very effective at helping us see through core stories related to illness, physical pain and suffering, and death.

Recognizing presence provides a peace that passes all understanding. No drug or addictive substance can provide this peace. So relapse is out of the question. Relapse during times of illness would only make sense if there were something lacking or something that needed to be escaped. When all energies are allowed to be just as they are, nothing needs to be covered up. There's nothing to escape.

In sickness and in health, presence is total and complete as it is. It seeks nothing. We easily dismiss the thought of relapse during these times. We bask in the light of presence instead. This is where our power lies.

Death

As we approach death, the peace of presence remains. Through resting in presence, we've come to see that the self-center we once took ourselves to be was never our true identity. The self-center was based on a fear of death. Presence releases this fear completely.

This unshakable knowing of what we are in the deepest sense allows us to die in complete acceptance.

We come to rest in peace in death, just as we rested in peace during life.

CHAPTER TEN: Misconceptions and Traps

This chapter deals with common traps and misconceptions about presence and about this way of recovery.

A misconception is essentially any mistaken view or attitude. Several of the misconceptions in this chapter arise from strongly intellectualizing presence or this way of recovery rather than taking up the practice of actually resting in presence.

There's a simple sweetness and well-being available to you through the practice of repeatedly relaxing into presence. It's something that can never be experienced merely through emphasizing beliefs or opinions about presence or about this way of recovery.

When we fully commit without reservation to the practice of resting in presence throughout the day, whenever possible, this sweetness and well-being become available to us.

This way of recovery is too simple and obvious to comprehend through the mind. When we try to figure it out with the mind and emphasize viewpoints about where we are on a time-bound path, we stay locked in self-centeredness and personal seeking. We miss the treasure available to us in restful presence.

Traps are places where we get stuck. By discussing these traps in this chapter, it may be easier to see them if they arise. In seeing them, we begin to be free of them.

Not everyone involved in this way of recovery will experience these misconceptions and traps. If any of these things arise for you, just revisit this chapter.

The Misconceptions and Traps

The Tendency to Measure Our Progress in Time

Before coming to the practice of presence, we lived with the habitual tendency to look to thoughts of the past and future for a sense of self. We consulted the past story to know who we are and emphasized the story of the future to know who we are becoming.

It makes perfect sense, *at first*, to treat recovery through presence the same way. We may find ourselves measuring back in time, saying things like, "I'm much more present than I was a year ago and I feel like I will learn to be even more present in the future." Again, at first, this is fine. It may actually empower us to continue making restful presence the most important thing in our lives.

But through resting in presence, we come to see that this measuring backward and forward is just more self-centeredness.

By noticing any thoughts that arise in some attempt to measure backward or forward in time, we take a moment to rest in presence. Present rest doesn't depend on anything that happened in the past. It also has nothing to do with any future moments of rest. To look to the future is to seek, even if we're looking for more rest in the future.

All sorts of interesting and profound spiritual experiences and states *may* arise through the practice of resting in presence. These experiences and states aren't a necessary part of recognizing presence, but they may accompany it. Some people experience them, some don't.

Past states and experiences are nothing more than memories appearing within presence. Future expectations about spiritual experiences and states are also nothing more than thoughts arising now.

Profound spiritual experiences and states aren't the goal here. States and experiences, no matter how positive or negative, are seen to be equal energies of presence. We enjoy positive experiences and states but we don't emphasize them for a sense of self.

The real power of natural rest lies in recognizing selfless presence as the stable, unchanging space in which all experiences, states, and other energies come and go equally as a dynamically, perfect flow.

This reveals to us incredible freedom and equanimity.

In restful presence, we see that measuring our progress in time simply isn't needed anymore. It becomes irrelevant. The sacredness of life is always here now.

Selfless presence carries a well-being that's never dependent on what happened before or what might happen later.

Presence Isn't Amnesia

It's a misconception to believe that presence is like amnesia. We don't lose our memories in presence.

Our stories remain fully available to us even once we see that these stories are not who we ultimately are. We continue to have a conventional self. A conventional self is a not a real, separate, permanent, objective self. That kind of self is unfindable. A conventional self is a play of ever-changing words, pictures and energy coming and going in the present moment. We don't deny these appearances coming and going. We just see that they never form anything real, separate, permanent or objective. We continue to use our names, remember our pasts, and have thoughts about the future. This way of recovery is about no longer *identifying* with these thoughts. It's not about getting rid of them or forgetting things about our personal histories.

Presence Isn't Escape

In first hearing of the practice of resting in presence and letting all energies come and go equally without emphasizing any of them, it may sound as if we're trying to escape life or whatever's appearing in life. This is a misconception, which usually comes from *thinking* about presence rather than the practice of resting in presence itself.

Let's take fear as an example. Whenever fear arises, it almost always relates to self-centered thought. The thoughts that accompany the fear refer to a self that feels threatened in some way. Whether we're thinking about an upcoming speech we have to give at work or knee replacement surgery, *it's all the same.* Fear keeps us trapped in a self-centered story.

This story doesn't really face anything. It tries to run away . . .

In this story, thought is working hard to cover up, get rid of, neutralize, or rationalize the fear. Thought plays out future scenarios, desperately looking for the scenario that says, "Everything will be okay." This is all an attempt to make the presently arising fear go away. This is the very definition of escape.

In presence, we're facing the suffering directly. We're looking at the thoughts that make up the story, seeing them for what they are—just thoughts arising and falling in restful presence. By bringing attention into the body where the raw energy of fear is arising, we're finally facing this fear that has been running our lives and fueling these thoughts.

In presence, we're not escaping things. We're facing them. We're seeing that each word, picture and energy is a temporary appearance only. Through presence, we're released from the drive to escape whatever's happening to us.

Although fear is being used as an example here, this applies to every thought, emotion, and sensation.

To face a thought or emotion doesn't mean to apply pressure toward it. It means to have no agenda about the thought or emotion. It means to have no desire to escape anything that arises. It means to allow all arisings to be exactly as they are, while resting in presence. This is about complete non-resistance to all energies, no matter what form they take.

When we turn to face what's arising, we find these energies aren't the big, bad monsters we thought they were. We find that presence is not in opposition to anything that arises. In this seeing, we discover that there's no self at the center of life.

All energies are seen to be equal movements of this selfless presence. In that seeing, the escaping stops.

Substitution

Substitution is a common trap. Substitution is the act of replacing one addictive substance or activity for another.

Here's an example:

Jill's addicted to meth but there are times when the drug isn't available. So she substitutes alcohol or pills.

There are also times when she tries to get clean on her own, without the help of any program. She goes for months at a time abstaining from drugs and alcohol completely. But during these abstinent periods, she finds herself preoccupied and even obsessed with issues surrounding weight loss, work, and boyfriends. She's again substituting.

After a period of abstinence from drugs and alcohol, Jill picks up meth again. She gets arrested and then placed in jail. While sitting in jail, she obsesses on her past and constantly thinks about what will happen to her in the future. She's substituting again. This time her drug of choice is excessive thinking.

She's released from prison and decides to get involved in a recovery program. In this program, Jill finds freedom from her desire to use drugs and alcohol, but also finds herself obsessed with money and shopping. Again, she's substituting. She works through those issues, and then becomes preoccupied with seeking self-improvement and spiritual awakening in the future. Another substitution.

To the mind, the content doesn't matter. Thought will obsess on any substance or activity including seeking spiritual awakening.

Although some substances or activities seem to be more addictive than others, when we look more closely, all addiction arises from the same Velcro Effect of words, pictures and energies feeling stuck together. No matter how much or how often we substitute one substance or activity for another, the structure's always the same. We're locked in a search for something else, something more.

In treating all substances and activities as equal, we are never disqualified from recovery. Natural rest helps release us from any and all addictions. We find no need to reach for a substitute when the seeking energy behind all addictions relaxes.

Confusing the Simple Enjoyment of Pleasure with Addiction/Compulsion

It may seem as if the goal of this way of recovery is to rid ourselves of the enjoyment of pleasure. But enjoying life's pleasures itself is not addiction.

Addiction is a repetitive, compulsive need for a particular substance or activity. For example, those who are not addicted to chocolate can eat it every now and then. They can *truly* take it or leave it! It's not a compulsion. They do not obsess on it. They do not have to have it every day or on some other repeated basis. They do not use it to medicate painful emotions. They simple enjoy it, moderately.

Compulsion is quite different. It's the sense of *having to have* a particular substance or engage in a particular activity, usually on a repeated basis (sometimes through binging). Addiction and compulsion is a way of trying to medicate painful feelings, escape a continuous sense of boredom or restlessness, or quiet excited or anxious thoughts or emotions. When there is a compulsion, we cannot simply "take or leave" that substance or activity. We HAVE to have it! Seeing the difference between addiction and the simple, occasional enjoyment of life's pleasures is critical to a healthy view of recovery.

Whatever you do, don't fool yourself! Recognize a compulsion for what it is. Notice when you can't just 'take or leave' a substance or activity. That's a compulsion.

Release the whole movement of compulsion itself using the practices and inquiries in this book. Let that be your first priority.

Don't deceive yourself into thinking that you are merely enjoying beer in the way that others enjoy an occasional brownie. Can you take or leave the beer? Are you using caffeine, drugs, food, or shopping to medicate feelings? That's the key to knowing whether there is an addiction present. If there is no compulsion, you should be able to enjoy certain pleasures in life with this "take it or leave it" attitude. Anything else is addiction.

Turning Natural Rest into Busy Work

This trap is related to substitution but it deserves its own discussion. In several chapters of this book, you'll find sets of inquiries and exercises. These practices help us question the thoughts that keep us locked in the cycle of replaying the past and seeking the future. This book also offers other practices, including shadow work and perspective taking.

None of these practices are meant to keep us busy thinking about ourselves all the time. This is about selfless presence, which is *freedom from the habitual tendency to focus on the self.*

The inquiries, exercises, shadow work, and perspective taking are designed to assist us in resting in presence on an ongoing basis. That's it! They're not designed to get us trapped in the cycle of seeking a better version of ourselves in the future or obsessing on busy spiritual work.

Shadow work is helpful only when we notice ourselves extremely bothered by or extremely attracted to a trait in someone else. If this isn't happening, then we completely forget about shadow work. We use it only when these things arise. We don't get busy looking around in our lives for all our shadows. That's just more seeking.

The same is true for the inquiries and exercises. If the inquiries and exercises aren't assisting us in resting in presence, then they have no value to us. In that case, they're becoming just another substitution, so we drop them.

In this way of recovery, we're only interested in present rest. If a spiritual practice isn't designed to awaken us to this moment, where freedom really is, it's probably just keeping us asleep within our self-centered story.

Compatible Practices

It may seem at first that resting in thought-free presence is incompatible with allowing all energies, including thoughts, to come and go freely.

In resting in thought-free presence, our aim isn't to suppress, destroy, or get rid of thought. We see that our real identity isn't any of the temporary thoughts or other energies that appear and disappear within the thought-free presence.

Through relaxing repeatedly into the natural rest of the present moment, we come to see that thought arises spontaneously and involuntarily. If, at any moment, we believe we have control over thoughts and other energies, then all we have to do is ask: "Do I know what energy movement will arise next? Do I know what my next thought will be?"

There's no way to know what thought or other energy movement will appear until it's already appeared. By that time, if we don't emphasize it and simply let it be as it is, we see that it's already on its way to disappearing. All energies are equal. They all do this. They arise spontaneously and involuntarily. They hang around for a while, and then disappear. When we make resting in presence the most important thing in our lives, none of these energies leave any trace.

Thoughts and all other energies are allowed to be just as they are. We no longer try to control this flow of energy.

We see that the natural rest of presence is the space in which all energies come and go. We see that resting in presence is perfectly compatible with allowing all energies to be as they are.

Story Mind vs. Functional Mind

Another viewpoint that can arise is the belief that presence will render us unable to function. We may believe that presence means we become dumb and unable to perform even simple life tasks.

This is a misconception. Again, it comes from emphasizing ideas about what presence might look like instead of actually taking up the practice of repeatedly resting in presence.

Through resting in presence, the self-centered story is seen through. The addictive cycle of personal seeking falls away. Thoughts are seen to be transparent. We're no longer identified with them. Functioning, however, continues perfectly.

To shed some light on this misconception, it may be helpful to make a distinction between story mind and functional mind.

In story mind, we're constantly seeking to gain something personally from the future, others, and situations. We act from a sense of lack or try to escape past negative feelings. We act from within a story, trying to control outcomes. In this story, the present moment is overlooked in favor of thoughts about the past and future. This stifles our ability to function effectively and with a clear mind.

In functional mind, we live and act from selfless presence. We're not looking to gain anything personally. We don't need anything. This moment contains perfect completeness.

Yet movement and functioning unfold intuitively within the stillness of presence, without a need to control outcomes. We find that all energies and movement arise spontaneously, causelessly, and dynamically as part of the natural flow of life. Whether we're talking to a friend, driving a car, or studying quantum physics, functioning happens effortlessly and effectively in presence.

We don't become perfect human beings. We see there's no such thing. Perfect functioning means living in the present moment without emphasizing the story that life should be the way we want it to be, or should unfold the way we believe it should unfold.

We see that the ideal of a perfect person was being sought only because we saw ourselves as deficient at the core. That false belief is seen through with the Unfindable and Boomerang Inquiries. We function more freely without that belief and the impossible standard it carries with it.

The Uniqueness of Each Person's Experience

As soon as they begin this way of recovery, some may find it very easy to rest in presence. Some may struggle at first and then find it easier once they stop being so hard on themselves.

If there's an initial struggle, it may be easier to take only very brief moments of rest many times throughout the day. The moments eventually become longer. Then at some point, there will be a natural return to presence that requires little to no effort.

Others may struggle against resting in presence for a more substantial period of time. The inability to rest in presence almost always comes from the habitual tendency to emphasize thoughts. These thoughts are often about: (1) how the past was better or worse than the present moment, (2) how the present moment isn't the way it's supposed to be, and/or (3) how the future will be better or worse.

It may be helpful to write out all these thoughts that are coming up regularly, that are making it difficult to rest. By putting them on paper, we may find it easier to spot these thoughts whenever they arise. This may allow us to rest more easily.

For those who are struggling a lot against the practice of resting in presence, the inquiries and shadow work can be helpful. Support and guidance from others are also beneficial. It can be worthwhile to start a mentoring relationship with a servant who has direct experience with overcoming this kind of struggle.

Some who come to this way of recovery may believe they're excluded from presence or that resting in presence is impossible for them. These are just temporary viewpoints coming and going within presence. They only seem true if we repeatedly emphasize them. No one is excluded from presence.

We take it easy on ourselves, letting the practice of presence unfold in its own way. We're not in a race toward the future. We're not in a race against others. We're simply becoming comfortable with the present moment in exactly the way it's appearing for us, even if its current appearance includes viewpoints about the difficulty of resting in presence.

Traps in Deep Rest

Some may never experience a period in which thought stops or slows down substantially. This is fine. The cessation of thought isn't necessary.

For these people, there may be no need to experience long periods of not thinking. They come to experience quietness and rest as underlying and permeating the movement of all energies. Thoughts either arise or they don't. Either way, there's no identification with them.

Others may experience a period in which thought substantially quiets. We call this "deep rest."

A "deep rest" period is a phase in which many concepts just stop appearing. The mind feels almost totally at rest. This "deep rest" may help some of us to disidentify from certain tightly held thoughts or beliefs that make up the core of the self-center. A deep rest period, however, isn't a requirement of this method.

In presence, we are truly at rest, whether thoughts and emotions are arising or not.

Through resting in presence, we find we no longer identify with thought and other temporary energies. That doesn't mean that thoughts must stop appearing.

In no longer identifying with thought (regardless of how that happens), we're freed from the cycle of addictive seeking.

Whether or not we experience a deep rest period, concepts that were once thought to be real may no longer appear real or true anymore. As we identify less with thought, the world may take on a dreamlike or unreal quality.

We want to be aware of any extreme viewpoints that may arise when identification with thought falls away. For example, there may be a tendency to emphasize such thoughts as, "There's no path to presence," "Nothing exists," or "All viewpoints are false."

These are also just viewpoints. There's nothing wrong with any viewpoint. But the freedom available here comes from restful presence, which is the space in which all viewpoints appear and disappear. The freedom doesn't come from emphasizing really spiritual-sounding ideas or extreme viewpoints.

All ideas are seen to be equal energies. This is good news. We come to see that no thought we emphasize can bring us closer to presence—and no thought can take us away from presence.

Each thought is seen to be like a breeze blowing through the air. It has no power to displace the air itself.

Those who do experience a deep rest period or disidentification from thought may experience confusion and frustration as one's personal motivation around certain issues begins to fall away. The personal viewpoints and other things that once motivated us to seek the future start to drop. This is fine! The self-center is being seen through. This is a normal phase that some people go through.

The confusion and frustration come from the last remnants of the addictive seeker, still looking for something else to happen. The old mechanism of personal seeking is still faintly operating. It appears in the form of subtle frustration in not knowing what to do next. It's often accompanied by a little voice that asks, "What's next?" This voice is still the addict talking. It's the seeker.

As our self-centered story is seen through and as our seeking toward future stops, selfless presence takes over. Selfless presence is realized when the voice, "What's next?" falls away or is no longer being emphasized.

In selfless presence, we have no idea how life is going to unfold. We have no interest in the question, "What's next?" We see the personal demand behind the question. We see that the question implies we're supposed to be in control or know what happens. With every demand on life, resistance is operating. When there's resistance to life, there's seeking toward the future for release.

When we resist what happens and try to control outcomes, we work against life. When we live in not knowing, having no personal demand on how things must unfold, life works through us.

Selfless presence is complete openness. In selfless presence, we aren't demanding that something else needs to happen. We live with open arms. A simple love of life resides in our hearts.

We remain open to whatever's happening and to whatever way life is actually unfolding. This is complete acceptance and surrender.

It's freedom from the addictive cycle of seeking. It's the beginning of living life in a totally new way (see *Chapter Ten: Selflessness*).

In deep rest, we aren't trying to get rid of thought permanently. The benefit of deep rest is only to disidentify from thought, not to kill the mind. It's not meant to escape life or the world. The mind continues to have a practical function in our lives, no matter how deeply we've realized that our real identity doesn't reside in thought.

Another trap that some people report during a deep rest period is detachment or even nihilism.

In deep rest, we want to notice any viewpoints that lead us to feel detached from what's happening, from life and other people.

Enjoying moments of quiet solitude is fine and can help us experience restful presence. But detaching from others is unhealthy. It arises as a result of a negative viewpoint or emotional resistance toward life, others, and/or the world. Detachment isn't selfless presence. It's another form of separation.

Deep rest is not "depressed." Depression comes from tuning out of our present, immediate experience and isolating back into the world of thoughts. It is a lack of intimacy with what is, a strategy of avoidance. Depression arises from emphasizing negative stories and not letting all emotions be as they are. Deep rest is a quiet mind that does not *identify* with thoughts and emotions as they pass through. In deep rest, anything and everything can arise, but we find no sense of self in anything that arises. This frees us to live fully but without our thoughts and emotions taking up our entire attention.

Through resting in presence, we come to see that we cannot truly separate ourselves from our present experience. And our present experience is life itself. Therefore, when we're buying into thoughts of detachment, we're buying into a false sense of separation between self and other, or self and life. We're hiding or trying to escape having to feel pain that may arise in relationships.

In noticing any thoughts of detachment, and resting in presence, we're already free of these thoughts of separation. In restful, thought-free presence, we're awake to the emotional resistance that's driving these viewpoints. In letting those emotional energies be as they are, the need to detach releases itself. We feel more and more comfortable in relationship.

Facing the suffering and conflict in relationship is precisely how we wake up from overreliance on divisive viewpoints and identification with the self-center. Relationship is not something to avoid. It's a vehicle through which we realize freedom.

We rest in alert, awake presence, welcoming our present situation as it is. Our communications with others are vibrantly alive, not deadened or pushed away in favor of silence. We're listening, living, and loving—not escaping into silence in order to avoid conflict or painful feelings. The quietness of presence is an opening, not a closing. It opens us to everything that's happening within and around us. If we begin to use presence as a way to close ourselves off, this is a sign that detachment is happening.

Nihilism is an extreme form of detachment that can arise, although it's rare. Nihilism is the belief that there's no meaning or purpose in life.

Don't mistake nihilism for spiritual awakening or presence. Nihilism is a belief system. If we experience nihilism, it means we're emphasizing thoughts about life being without purpose or meaning. These are viewpoints based on a resistance to life. In noticing them as nothing more than viewpoints, we can be free of them.

Presence isn't about detaching from life or the world. It's not about living in a story that life is meaningless. It's about disidentifying from thought, emotion, and other energies that arise and fall. This happens automatically and effortlessly through resting in presence.

Detachment and disidentification are two totally different things. We don't want to confuse them. Let's revisit the pond metaphor from *Chapter One* to explain the difference.

Restful, selfless presence is like the pond. The energies that come and go within presence are the same as ripples across the pond's surface. The pond and the ripples are inseparable. The ripples are all the thoughts, emotions, sensations, people, situations, and relationships that come and go within presence. To deny life in all its diverse appearances is to deny presence itself.

Trying to push away these energies is like a pond trying to push away its own ripples.

Detachment happens when we take a negative attitude toward the ripples. We try to keep from experiencing the world of ripples, pushing them all away. This comes from personal will. *In detachment, we're at war with what is.*

In disidentification, we carry no resistance toward the ripples. As the pond, we allow each ripple to be as it is. We see that each ripple is temporary. So no ripple can define or move the pond.

Whereas detachment carries negative feelings of loneliness, sadness, or apathy, disidentification reveals a natural peace, freedom, well-being, and equanimity, available in every moment.

Presence is the realization that we're inseparable from life, from others, and from whatever's happening in life.

Presence is love, not detachment.

Presence Isn't Stagnancy

If we emphasize viewpoints about presence rather than experientially resting in presence, we may imagine that presence is about stagnancy. Stagnancy is a state of not developing, flowing, or changing. This is another misconception about presence.

Again, the pond metaphor is helpful here. Presence is like the deep, still pond that's always changelessly at rest. We rely on this presence completely. It provides unshakable mental and emotional stability. In this rest, we find freedom from the cycle of addictive seeking.

But this stability isn't stagnancy. In presence, we're not stuck in a state where nothing happens or where we oppose change. Life continues happening. The ripples continue flowing across the surface of the pond and are seen to be inseparable from the pond.

Life contains a radical diversity of energies including thoughts, emotions, states, sensations, experiences, people, relationships, perspectives, families, and careers. We come to see these as temporary, illusive movements within presence.

In this way of recovery, we're not disengaging or denying this fluid flow of diversity and change. This flow has no independent existence from presence. We embrace life fully. We see ourselves as life itself appearing as this perfect flow of diverse energies.

We experience a deepening in presence. As more and more self-centered viewpoints are seen through, a deeper surrender is available. This deepening isn't the self-center engaged in its usual game of personal seeking. Seeking comes from emphasizing thoughts about the future; it's based in a present sense of lack.

Deepening is different. It comes from seeing through those viewpoints and being able to relax effortlessly into the natural rest of the present moment. Deepening is a movement of selflessness. It opens us up more and more to the natural abundance within us and all around us and to the completeness of the present moment.

In the present moment, life unfolds in a mysterious way. We never know what's going to happen next. We simply remain open to the constantly changing energies flowing within presence.

In selfless presence, we may still achieve, grow, learn, and evolve over time. We may still explore new opportunities, advance in our jobs, and be successful in the world, if that's what appeals to us. Presence doesn't outlaw anything. Presence is an opening, not a closing.

The difference is there's no personal seeking behind these movements. The present moment remains primary, always.

In presence, we aren't looking to the future for personal fulfillment. This allows us to be fully here in the present moment. It leaves us open to explore the unfolding of life without personal expectations. In no longer looking to the future for personal fulfillment, we may even continue to have goals but they are held more lightly, without an attachment to any particular outcome or course of action. We're content no matter how life unfolds within this present space.

Selfless presence leaves us open to create in the world . . . in a whole new way.

We open ourselves up to possibilities that aren't available whenever we're operating from a self-centered story of lack.

When we live from lack, we only want to take. Our creative energy is stifled. We're always seeking personal gain. This narrows our vision. We look at the world with self-centered tunnel vision. We live in a cycle of personal seeking toward the future.

Selfless presence is abundance. When we live in abundance, we seek nothing for ourselves. We experience contentment simply for being alive. We only want to give and be open to whatever unfolds in the next moment. We're truly open to positive change, for others, the world, and ourselves. Yet, we remain unattached to outcomes.

Making Presence into a Thing

Reading words like "presence" so often in this book, or other words like "natural rest," can lead to making words into things. The mind only thinks in terms of objects. So it is natural that it would think of presence as a thing. This can lead to dogmatic thinking where presence is defended or treated like a religion. Be careful of this tendency. The easiest way to see that presence is not a thing the mind can grasp is to use the UI. Try to find presence. Is the word "presence" it? No, that's just a word. How about that peaceful feeling or sensation you feel. Is that it? No, that is a feeling or something you sense. Keep looking . . . Presence is as unfindable as any object you try to find using the UI. Do yourself a favor and use the UI on any word on which you find yourself stuck. Be free of all dogmatic thinking. That kind of deep freedom cannot be realized by hanging onto such concepts.

CHAPTER ELEVEN: Selflessness

This chapter describes the transformation we discover through natural rest.

The natural rest of presence has obvious benefits. The words in this chapter are not intended as dangling carrots that pull us into more seeking towards future. These benefits are realized through the recognition of timeless, selfless freedom. As described in the last chapter, the benefits arise from *deepening into this present recognition*, not seeking some later point in your time-bound story.

In this deepening, we see through the self-center, which is the time-bound story.

Selflessness reveals itself naturally in this recognition.

In this selflessness, we're no longer attached to images within the story of self. We're free of attachment to the past as well as the future. We're no longer attached to the identity of being a separate person, totally cut off from others and the world.

The memory of our past is still available. The future continues to unfold. But our sense of identity is no longer found in thoughts of the past or future.

We live in simple, timeless being.

The present moment remains primary in all situations. We find that acceptance and surrender aren't things that we *do*. Rather, they're natural attributes available in presence.

We're no longer guided by guilt, sadness, depression, or anxiety. We no longer believe that we're a conceptual label. No label from the past sticks at this point, including the label "addict" or even "recovering addict."

Self-centered thoughts may still arise but we're no longer identified with them.

Thoughts, emotions, cravings, states, and sensations that once remained unseen, and that once fueled our seeking, are now seen. They no longer have power over us.

We experience life as a seamless flow. A moment of rest feels seamlessly inseparable from a movement of energy and vice versa.

All energies are seen to be inseparable and equal appearances of presence.

We find a seamless balance between all energies.

We feel at home in the present moment and experience equanimity and well-being regardless of what else is happening.

We see through the dualism of the mind. We no longer find ourselves attached to one side of a pair of opposites, like right vs. wrong, positive vs. negative, or black vs. white. We're open to seeing and embracing each side.

We find that thought still arises but it's experienced as lighter, more transparent, quieter, more in the background, and much less personal than it was in our seeking days.

As thought feels less personal, the sense of separation between self and other people and things relaxes. We respect conventional boundaries, but we live in a loving, compassionate, and undivided way in *all* relationships.

We welcome all viewpoints as they appear. Thought is allowed to come and go, without ever forming a separate self.

Emotions have no ability to torture us anymore. They come and they go. They leave no trace.

Each thought, emotion, craving, sensation, state, and experience comes and goes effortlessly, spontaneously, and causelessly.

Each movement is uninterruptedly allowed to arise and fall. Each movement of energy disappears into the still, quiet space of presence.

The personal will that was trying to control all that energy falls away.

Selfless presence stops looking like a practice and more like what we are in the most basic sense.

Life lives itself through us.

We realize fully that we don't know what's going to happen next. This *not knowing* provides unconditional freedom. We see that we *never* knew what was going to happen, even in the days of personal seeking when we used to be attached to outcomes. We were living a lie!

We effortlessly allow everything to be as it is. We allow the future to unfold without trying to control how it unfolds.

We lose the desire to use addictive substances and engage in addictive activities. We know that the only reason we were using these substances and activities in our seeking days is because we were looking for our freedom.

Selfless presence contains a natural well-being and freedom that no drug or other addictive substance can ever bring. This is why we're free of the need to relapse.

Drugs and addictive activities are poor substitutes for the well-being and freedom of presence.

Cravings all but disappear. And if they appear, they have no charge. Without a charge, they disappear, leaving no trace.

Obsession loses its control over us. It greatly diminishes or stops arising altogether. If obsession appears, it's noticed immediately. We see it arises in a presence that allows it to be completely as it is. In this awareness, obsession loses its ability to continue.

In presence, our contentment, freedom, and peace are uncaused and unconditional. We no longer believe that other people and things hold the key to our contentment, freedom, or peace.

We no longer believe that seeking something else in the future is necessary for contentment. No temporary substance or activity can add to a timeless freedom and well-being that's total and complete as it is.

We're free to experience this moment with fresh eyes and ears and with a heart fully open to each experience, each person, each viewpoint.

We're unafraid of and unattached to outcomes. Without expectations, every moment is a gift—a welcomed guest, perfect just as it is.

By "perfect," we don't mean that conflicts no longer arise or that challenging situations like divorce, unemployment, physical pain, illness, and death don't occur. These things may occur.

Perfect, in this sense, means that presence provides a natural and limitless capacity to fully face, but not identify with, the thoughts and emotions that appear in these situations. Even during challenging times, we experience an undercurrent of well-being.

This well-being permeates every moment. We no longer seek to alter our moods with addictive substances or activities. We no longer chase after pleasant feelings in avoidance of pain that may arise in challenging situations.

We no longer need an outside fix. We have inner peace, contentment, and freedom.

In selfless presence, we realize a naturally occurring gratitude that's present simply because we're alive. This gratitude isn't tied to things we acquire or to what we hope might happen in the future. It isn't dependent on circumstances or situations.

In selfless presence, we notice the simple wonders of life that escaped us when we were trapped in constant seeking toward the future.

We notice the feel of a breeze on our faces, the sound of traffic, a bird singing outside our window, the voice of a friend and his story, or the sheer gratitude for simply breathing and being alive.

We enjoy the simplicity of whatever's appearing *in this moment.*

We find that life is and was always here, in the present moment, waiting for us to discover it beyond our self-centered, time-bound stories.

No longer identifying with our self-centered story doesn't mean that presence erases individuality.

We retain our individual talents, skills, knowledge, and other unique attributes. We find that we each bring something unique to relationships and to life. We cherish this uniqueness.

In seeing through the self-center, we no longer use these attributes for selfish gain, or as a way to feel better or more special than others.

We utilize these attributes in a selfless way for the benefit of everyone. This takes no effort, planning, control, or manipulation. It happens naturally and effortlessly through the simple recognition of presence.

In selfless presence, we find no need for hope. We see that hope was based only on seeking.

Hope is based on the idea that the present moment lacks something and that this lack will be filled in the future. In selfless presence, there's no lack, so there's no longer a need for hope.

In recognizing selflessness, the personal search for something more ends. We discover an uncontrived, unconditional presence that isn't dependent on any experience and, yet, permeates every experience.

Presence lacks nothing, so the search for something more in the future naturally falls away. Yet, we remain completely open to learning and to life's constant unfolding.

We see that the viewpoints, "I have arrived at spiritual awakening," and "I have not arrived yet" are equal energies of presence. We don't have to emphasize either viewpoint for a sense of self. We simply live as what we really are—presence.

We remain open to taking multiple perspectives and to re-owning shadows whenever they appear, to seeing where we may get stuck in a particular viewpoint that separates us from others. In seeing where we're stuck, we awaken again to the possibility of remaining completely open, compassionate, and loving.

Each moment is its own awakening.

In taking the perspectives of others, we're better able to see life from the viewpoints of our sons, daughters, spouses, partners, co-workers, bosses, family members, and people from other political parties, religions, philosophies, or countries.

This creates compassion and harmony. It heals any damaged relationships from our past.

We expect nothing in return for our actions in our relationships. No longer do we take action in order to receive a personal benefit.

We no longer expect people to do or say what we want them to do or say. Each person that comes within our presence is allowed to be exactly as they are.

Each moment is accepted exactly as it is.

When we remain open to the present moment in this way, we find our calling in life.

At a minimum, we operate in each moment in natural, selfless, timeless acceptance. When we're engaged in projects that excite us, we experience a vibrant, alive inspiration and enthusiasm.

As the addictive seeking energy dissolves through this way of recovery, all that's left is our natural energy. It becomes freely available to us in the here and now.

Life's no longer a chore. It's a gift.

In selflessness, the question, "What benefits everyone?" becomes an aspect of our very being. Wisdom and compassion arise naturally in each situation. We live to be of service.

Being of service comes naturally and effortlessly in selflessness. It never feels like work.

In selflessness, love takes action through us. Love is recognizing itself everywhere, in every person we encounter.

When the self-center falls away, we want to help others.

We find ourselves wanting to be engaged in our communities. We get involved with causes that benefit others. This happens naturally, as a result of no longer being self-centered.

Selfless presence includes being fully engaged with life. It's seeing that we are life itself, aware of itself, and taking care of itself . . . in every area.

We experience life as an unchanging, stable, selfless presence in which the dynamic flow of change naturally occurs.

Each moment is experienced as completely fresh, revealing that whatever arises is only temporary. It is not who we are. The past and future no longer rule our experience. Emotional pain becomes the way into freedom instead of something to escape.

Addiction is no longer seen as a death sentence or even a life sentence. It becomes the doorway to present freedom through rest and inquiry.

Recovery never has to be about seeking the future again. It's always about seeing that this moment lacks nothing and that there is nothing to seek. In this moment-by-moment seeing, we remain open to look into any self-centered stories that may pop up from time to time and to undo any Velcro Effect with the Living Inquiries. That's not seeking. That's present looking.

Always keep recovery simple: ***Rest*** in the midst of whatever is happening. ***Inquire*** when needed. And . . . ***Enjoy life!***

Acknowledgments

Special thanks to the following: Chad for his undying love and support, Mom, Dad, Mark, Teri, Kevin, Jolinda Kirby, preliminary editors Z and Scotty Rathjen, primary editor C.J. Schepers for her amazing editing touch, Curt King for all his work above and beyond the call of duty, Bart McFarlane for his devotion and attention to all things related to Natural Rest and for final editing work that really enhanced the book, Jeff Foster for the Foreword, Greg Goode for being such an amazing teacher and friend, Ken Wilber for permission to use the 3-2-1 Process, Chris Hebard for his enthusiasm, insight and love of the topic of recovery, my friends from the NA fellowship for helping me in the beginning of recovery, and David Langer and John Raatz for their help and creativity in the beginning. Special thanks to Colette Kelso for co-developing the Compulsion Inquiry with me. What a great tool! Thanks to the Living Inquiries Senior Facilitators and Trainers for their devoted attention to further development of the inquiries. No act is done alone. No man or woman is an island onto him- or herself. Without the support of these people and so many others, this book would never have made it into the hands of a single reader. These are the people who have graciously and selflessly given me the support and space I needed to write this book. Thank you, from the deepest place in my heart!

Other Books by Scott Kiloby

The Unfindable Inquiry

Living Realization: Your Present Experience As It Is

Doorway to Total Liberation: Conversations with What Is

Reflections of the One Life: Daily Pointers to Enlightenment

Love's Quiet Revolution: The End of the Spiritual Search

Scott Kiloby's Web Sites

Scott's web site containing information relevant to addiction and recovery:
www.naturalrestforaddiction.com

Scott's main site:
www.kiloby.com

Scott's site on the Living Inquiries:
www.livinginquiries.com

Made in the USA
Lexington, KY
15 March 2014